BRIGHT NOTES

BAAL AND OTHER WORKS BY BERTOLT BRECHT

Intelligent Education

INFLUENCE PUBLISHERS

Nashville, Tennessee

BRIGHT NOTES: Baal and Other Works
www.BrightNotes.com

ISBN: 978-1-645424-24-6 (Paperback)
ISBN: 978-1-645424-25-3 (eBook)

Originally published by Monarch Press.
William P. Kenney, 1965
2020 Edition published by Influence Publishers.

Interior design by Lapiz Digital Services. Cover Design by Thinkpen Designs.

Printed in the United States of America.

Library of Congress Cataloging-in-Publication Data forthcoming.
Names: Intelligent Education
Title: BRIGHT NOTES: Baal and Other Works
Subject: STU004000 STUDY AIDS / Book Notes

CONTENTS

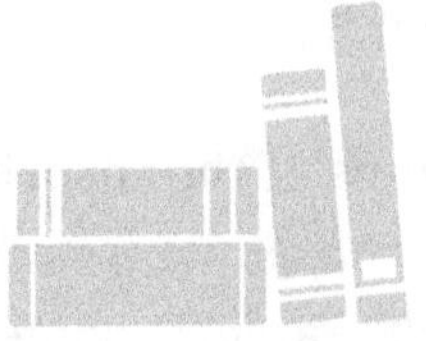

BERTOLT BRECHT

INTRODUCTION

PREFACE

Few figures in the modern theatre have aroused as much interest and discussion as the German playwright Bertolt Brecht. Brecht's influence, both as an artist and as theoretician, continues to be felt throughout the world. This study guide is undertaken with the hope of aiding the reader in the study of some of Brecht's major works and of suggesting the nature of Brecht's importance for the modern theater and for modern literature and thought in general.

The guide is divided into five major parts. The first, introductory section includes a brief summary of the major events of Brecht's life and a discussion of his theories of the theater. Brecht's theories have received such widespread attention that many readers who are all but totally unfamiliar with his plays can speak knowledgeably of his theories. This is an unhealthy situation and one that Brecht would deplore. While some knowledge of Brecht's is desirable, it is secondary to an understanding and appreciation of his plays. It is especially unwise, and false to Brecht's theory intentions, to read the plays as mere illustrations of the theories. In fact, the reader is advised not to concern himself with Brecht's theory until he has read, and read thoroughly, at least some of the major plays. Our most profound attention must be reserved, not for Brecht the theoretician, but for Brecht the playwright.

In the present guide Brecht the playwright is most fully represented in the second and longest section. This consists of summaries of and comments upon ten of Brecht's dramatic works. The summaries aim to present clearly and concisely the major action of the plays. The comments deal with matters of structure and meaning and with analysis of major characters.

The plays are analyzed in the order in which they were written, but five are singled out for especially detailed consideration. Of these, four - *Mother Courage, Galileo, The Good Woman of Setzuan*, and *The Caucasian Chalk Circle*, are generally regarded as Brecht's masterworks, and the fifth - *The Threepenny Opera* - has been his greatest popular success. All ten plays chosen for analysis are readily available in English translation; it is hoped that interest in Brecht is not limited to students of German.

The third section of the guide consists of a short critical discussion of Brecht's work as a whole. This discussion attempts to suggest the overall design of Brecht's career, pointing out recurring **themes** and techniques and indicating evidences of change and development in the various periods of Brecht's life.

A fourth section of the guide includes a series of study questions, aimed at helping the reader to review Brecht's work. Finally, a fifth section contains an annotated bibliography, suggesting where the reader may find the most important works on Brecht available in English.

This guide is in no way intended as a substitute for the plays themselves. Reading of the analysis of any play should follow intensive reading, and precede intensive rereading, of the play itself. It is with the plays that we begin and to them that we must return.

A NOTE ON FORMAT

In the section of the guide devoted to analysis of the plays, the first title given for each play is that by which it is best known in English, after which the original German title and alternate English titles will be found in parentheses.

THE LIFE AND CAREER OF BERTOLT BRECHT

Many of the changes that have helped to shape the modern world and the issues that have divided it are reflected in the eventful life of Bertolt Brecht. Born in the united Germany of Bismarck's Reich, he died in the divided Germany of the Cold War. The offspring of bourgeois parents, he allied himself with the revolutionary forces of his age and spent his last years in Communist East Berlin. To this day, the nature of Brecht's allegiance to communism remains a matter of speculation. That he turned his back on the West is clear; but whether he had any real hope in the East is uncertain. At any rate, Brecht's ambiguous relationship to the central political issues of his time - and ours - is one source of his continuing fascination for us.

EARLY LIFE

Born February 10, 1898, in Augsburg, Germany, Brecht was christened Eugen Berthold Friedrich Brecht. Brecht always disliked this elongated name, and as a young man took to calling himself Bertolt - or Bert-Brecht, which he seems to have considered simpler, less pretentious, and stronger than the name his parents had chosen for him.

Brecht was born into a period of great change in Germany, which was embarked on the path of industrialization that has been the basis of its power in the present century. Yet Augsburg in 1898 was still a quiet city, and Brecht's parents were prosperous members of its respectable middle class. His father was the managing director of a local paper mill, and his mother was the daughter of a civil servant. Brecht was baptized in the Protestant faith of his mother, although his father was Catholic.

Brecht's education was conventional enough. He attended a public elementary school from 1904 to 1908, and from 1908 to 1917, he was a student at the Realgymnasium (academic high school) in Augsburg. In 1917 he entered the University of Munich as a medical student, but he was called up for military service the following year.

In the army, Brecht served as a medical orderly. His military experiences seem to have had a great effect on him. His firsthand look at the horrors of war reinforced the pacifistic views he had already been forming as a student, and pacifism was to remain an important element of his thought for the rest of his life.

The Germany to which Brecht returned after the war was a defeated, disturbed, and disordered land, and there is no reason to suspect that the attractions of communism first suggested themselves to Brecht at this time. Communism enjoyed a brief period of dominance in Bavaria following the Russian Revolution in 1918, and Brecht found himself a member of the Augsburg Revolutionary Committee. In spite of the sympathy with communism this suggests, Brecht was by no means firmly committed to communism at this time.

EARLY DRAMATIC WORKS

In 1920 Brecht, who had already written his first play, *Baal,* arrived in Munich. Two years later his play *Trommeln in der Nacht (Drums in the Night)* was produced there, and led to Brecht's receiving the Kleist Prize, an award given annually to the best young dramatic talent, in 1922. In the same year Brecht married Marianne Zoff; this marriage ended in divorce five years later.

In the course of the 1920s, Brecht gained wide experience in the various aspects of the theater. He held the post of "Dramaturg" (a mixture of dramatic adviser, editor, and public-relations man) in the Munich Kammerspiele theater in 1920, and later worked with Max Reinhardt and Erwin Piscator, two of the great German producers of the period. The work of Piscator in particular influenced Brecht's developing theories of the theater.

Meanwhile Brecht continued to write. Among his more important plays of the 1920s are *In the Swamp* (1923) and *A Man's a Man* (1926). In 1928 Brecht collaborated with the composer Kurt Weill in *In The Threepenny Opera*, which proved to be his greatest popular success. There is considerable **irony** in the fact that his work was much enjoyed by Germany's middle class, who, failing to understand Brecht's dark comedy, were not aware that their values were under attack.

By 1930 Brecht had apparently moved from the nihilism implied by plays like *In the Swamp* to a commitment to communism. This commitment received dramatic expression in one of Brecht's most powerful and disturbing plays, *The Measures Taken*, which was completed in 1930. Also completed in this year were *The Rise and Fall of the City of Mahagonny*, again in collaboration with Weill, and *St. Joan of the Stockyards*. In the same year Brecht was working on an adaptation of *Mother*, a novel by the Russian writer Maxim Gorky.

EXILE

By this time the Nazi threat was becoming increasingly clear, and when Hitler gained power in 1933, Brecht decided it was time to leave Germany. He and his family (he had married the actress Helene Weigel in 1928) emigrated to Scandinavia, settling in Denmark until the summer of 1939. In view of Brecht's Communist beliefs, some writers have wondered why Brecht chose exile in Denmark rather than in the Soviet Union, and have suggested that perhaps Brecht's intellectual commitment to communism did not blind him to communism's many shortcomings in practice - at least as it was practiced in Stalin's Russia.

BRECHT IN THE UNITED STATES

By 1939 Hitler's shadow was spreading across Europe, and Brecht decided to leave Denmark. He lived for a while in Stockholm, Sweden, and then in Finland. Finally, in July, 1940, he entered the United States. Again, his choice of a home in exile is interesting. To get from Finland to San Francisco, Brecht had to travel across Russia. We are bound to wonder why this supposedly committed Communist was unwilling to remain in the Communist's "paradise." Perhaps, in spite of his commitment,

Brecht was unwilling at this time to accept the limits on artistic freedom that he could expect in Stalin's totalitarian state.

The 1930s were productive years for Brecht. His adaptation of Gorky's *Mother* was completed and produced, but public performances of it were banned in Germany in 1932. In 1938 he completed his anti-Nazi play *The Private Life of the Master Race.*

The year 1939 marks the beginning of Brecht's richest creative period. In this year he completed two of his greatest works, the first version of *Galileo* (a second version, for American production, was completed in 1947) and *Mother Courage*. A third major work, *The Good Woman of Setzuan*, was completed in 1941. Brecht completed his fourth unquestioned masterpiece, *The Caucasian Chalk Circle*, in 1945.

In addition to these major works, Brecht produced several other dramatic pieces in the early 1940s. The most controversial of these is probably *The Resistible Rise of Arturo Ui*, an attempt to portray the career of Adolf Hitler by an analogy to Chicago gangsterism. The word "resistible" (aufhaltsame) is of special significance, for Brecht rejected the so-called tragic vision which sees the kind of evil represented by Hitler as inevitable. It need not have happened, Brecht cries out. Man, he insists, can make a better world if he seriously chooses to do so.

While in the United States, Brecht supported himself financially by working on a number of film scripts for Hollywood studios. On the whole, Brecht felt that his work was distorted in the films to which he contributed. The most distinguished film to which he devoted his talents is probably *Hangman Also Die*, set in Czechoslovakia during the German occupation of that country. The film was brilliantly directed by Brecht's great compatriot and fellow exile, Fritz Lang; but again, Brecht was dissatisfied with what was done to his script in the final version of the film.

In 1947 Brecht's *Galileo* received its first American production, which was not a popular success, but it seems to have been an artistic one. The production was directed by Joseph Losey, who has since earned an international reputation as a film director, and featured Charles Laughton, who was also primarily responsible for the English adaptation, in the title role.

Brecht's political opinions led in 1947 to an appearance before the House Un-American Activities Committee. In parrying the Committee's questions, Brecht played a role not unlike that he assigned to Galileo in his play. At any rate, the committed Communist seemed to fool the professional Communist-hunters. "He is doing all right," said the Committee chairman. "You are a good example," he told Brecht. The following year Brecht moved to East Berlin.

THE LAST YEARS

While in Berlin Brecht completed his *Little Organon for the Theatre*, the fullest statement of his dramatic theories. He was also active in the Berliner Ensemble, a theatrical group, staging productions of his own plays and of those of others.

If Brecht had any criticisms to make of the more restrictive features of East Germany's Communist government, he never made them in public. In fact, he became prized by the Communists as an example of the "superiority" of Communist culture. He was awarded the East German National Prize in 1951 and the Stalin Peace Prize in 1954. But in spite of the position of honor he held,

Brecht on several occasions had difficulties with East German censorship.

Brecht's last years brought with them much that might have brought him satisfaction. The importance of his work was coming to be recognized all over the world. He had the opportunity to work with a brilliant company of actors. Yet he also suffered the frustrations of the creative artist in an authoritarian society. We may never know with any assurance whether Brecht was satisfied that these frustrations were justified by the Communist ideal. Bertolt Brecht died of coronary thrombosis in August, 1956. He left behind a mass of manuscripts, including diaries. What he may have confided to these diaries, and whether the government of East Germany will ever permit them to be published, remain matters of doubt.

THE THEATER OF BRECHT

Brecht's Theory of Theater

In any discussion of Brecht's theory, it is important at all times to remember that he was always a practical man of the theatre, rather than an academic always aesthetician. His practical bias reveals itself in his willingness to modify his theory in the light of experience and to ignore theory entirely when it seemed irrelevant to the practical problems of an individual production. It must be kept in mind, then, that the theory discussed below grew out of many years of practical experience in the theater. A summary of Brecht's key ideas, which is all that can be attempted here, does not do justice to the flexibility characteristic of Brecht's mind. Brecht's ideas developed and changed in the course of his life and would certainly have continued to do so if he had lived longer.

Furthermore, Brecht's theory did not develop in a vacuum. A full understanding of Brecht's theory would require something that this guide cannot do, namely, an understanding of the German theater against which Brecht reacted in his theory and practice.

Finally, the reader is reminded once again that the relation between Brecht's theory and practice is uncertain and ambiguous. The plays are not written merely to illustrate the theory, and the theory can only partially explain what happens in the plays. Still, some knowledge of Brecht's theory will probably prove useful in understanding what might otherwise seem strange in the plays.

The Theater of Illusion

If Brecht's plays do seem strange to us, it is perhaps because we are accustomed to the **conventions** of the "theater of illusion." The basic **convention** of this theater is that what we are watching on the stage is life itself. It is as though we look into a room, the fourth wall of which has magically been rendered invisible. No device which may shatter this illusion, such as a direct address to the audience, is permitted. Sets, lighting, make-up, and acting are all designed to intensify this illusion.

Accustomed as we have become to the theater of illusion, we sometimes make the mistake of concluding that it is the only way of true theater. Yet the theater of illusion has played only a small part in the history of the theater as a whole. The theater of Shakespeare, for example, with its blank verse, its soliloquies, and its simplified staging has little to do with the theater of illusion.

Anti-Illusionist Theater

Many modern playwrights have recognized the limitations of the theater of illusion and have presented alternatives to it. In the American theater, Eugene O'Neill's *Strange Interlude*, Thornton Wilder's *Our Town*, Tennessee Williams' *The Glass Menagerie*, and Arthur Miller's *Death of a Salesman* are but a few of the many important plays that in some degree reject illusionist conventions. European rebels against illusionism include such significant figures as Luigi Pirandello in Italy, Erwin Piscator (with whom Brecht worked) in Germany, and, more recently, Samuel Beckett, Eugene Ionesco, and Jean Genet in France.

Brecht was not alone, then, in rejecting the **conventions** of the theater of illusion. We shall now examine some of the specific terms of Brecht's rebellion.

STRUCTURE

According to Brecht, the traditional dramatic form is based on artificial and unnecessary restrictions. The play deals with a single action, is limited in the range of time and space it covers, and each scene is important only for what it contributes to the whole. As an alternative (and the ability to see alternatives is of central importance in Brecht's thought) Brecht suggests an "**epic**" structure - that is, a structure based on the epic, a looser, narrative form, which is of its nature episodic and in which each **episode** is significant, not only for what it contributes to the whole, but in itself.

The **epic** differs further from the dramatic form in that, as narrative, it deals with past events (expressed in the past tense), rather than with the imaginary "present" of the drama, which unfolds before us as if it were happening for the first time. In his "**epic**" theater, Brecht wants the audience to see the action as something that has happened in the past, in a particular time and place, and that is now being re-enacted. Again, the audience is not permitted the illusion that what is on the stage is life in the process of being lived.

STAGING

The "**epic**" structure in itself is only one part of Brecht's theory. The implications of the structure must be realized in the staging. Brecht was less interested than many of his contemporaries in changing the shape of the stage, or the physical relationship of stage to auditorium (as in arena theater, where a circular stage is placed in the center of the auditorium). What he wanted to change was the relationship between the audience and what happens on the stage. The audience must not be hypnotized into accepting the theatre as "real." Since part of the hypnotic effect of the contemporary theater is derived from the darkened state of the auditorium, Brecht often argued that the lights in the auditorium should remain lit. In this way, the audience would remain fully conscious, intellectually alert, as he wished them to be. They would be better able to judge what goes on on the stage, rather than merely accepting it passively as so often occurs.

Brecht also insisted that the devices used on stage should not be aimed at fooling the audience into forgetting that they are in a theater. If a scene is set at night, simply hang up an artificial moon to indicate that it is night, rather than using artificial lighting to create the illusion that it really is night. Let the stage always be bathed in brilliant light, so that the audience may see clearly all that is happening. In his early writing, Brecht even insisted that the sources of light themselves should be placed in clear view of the audience, but he later modified this idea when experience taught him that it resulted in undesirable distraction.

A similar anti-illusionist intention is revealed in Brecht's attitude toward other elements of stage productions. The kind of set which attempts to reproduce in complete illusionist detail a real place was repugnant to him. He preferred a simplified stage that did not pretend to be anything but a stage. The contrast between this simplified stage and the reality of particular objects, such as the wagon of *Mother Courage*, was an important part of Brecht's theater. It encouraged the audience to see the significance of the important objects, rather than passively contemplating a pseudo-reality. Brecht's attitude towards such details as costuming and make-up is consistent with this basic position.

ACTING

In Brecht's theater, as in all theater, the actor is of supreme importance. What is unusual in Brecht's theater is that Brecht argues against the actor's becoming the character he plays. It is the actor's job to "demonstrate" the character. In an important passage Brecht clarifies this idea by comparing the actor to an onlooker who is describing an accident he has witnessed. Occasionally, the onlooker finds it necessary to "act" - to show us what the people involved in the accident - say, the pedestrian struck by an automobile - did. We do not confuse the onlooker with the pedestrian. While remaining clearly himself, the onlooker demonstrates what the pedestrian did. He acts out, or demonstrates, the pedestrian's walk, his failure to look both ways before stepping off the curb, and so on. So should the actor, while remaining clearly himself, demonstrate what the character did. Thus Peter Lorre, in the original production of *Mann Ist Mann*, remained Peter Lorre while demonstrating the behavior of Galy Gay. The traditional way of praising an actor - "He's not playing Lear, he is Lear" - has no place in Brecht's scale of theatrical values.

ALIENATION

One of the most widely discussed elements of Brecht's theory is his concept of alienation, a concept implicit in almost all the other elements of the theory. In the original German Brecht's word for his concept is verfremdung, sometimes translated as "estrangement." It refers essentially to a process of forcing the audience to see things in a new light, to "alienate" or "estrange" the audience from what has become familiar to it.

The idea of alienation is by no means completely original with Brecht. The English Romantic poet Shelley is one of many who have defined the poet's task as making us look upon familiar people, objects, and situations as if seeing them for the first time, when they were first strange to us. Brecht points out that one becomes in this sense "alienated" from one's mother when she remarries. One sees her then in a new light, as another man's wife, and it is almost as though one had never seen her before.

The idea of "alienation," then, is not new in itself. What is new is the emphasis Brecht places on its social implications. When we have become completely accustomed to anything, it is an easy matter to assume that it has always been so, that it will always be so. That is, we accept the inevitability of what we are used to. But when something new is offered to us, we recognize that it is not inevitable, that we may accept or reject it. Now, when we are "alienated" from something that is familiar, it is as though that something were new. It looks strange to us, and we are forced to recognize that a thing so new and strange is not inevitable, and therefore that it could be otherwise. For Brecht, this applies as well to social, political, and economic systems as to anything else. The artist who "alienates" capitalism, for instance, invites the audience to see that there are alternatives to capitalism, that it need not be taken for granted; it could be otherwise. As Brecht sees it, the demonstration by "alienation" that society can be changed must lead the audience to change it along Communist lines. This conclusion does not, however, follow logically from anything else in Brecht's theory and will not seem convincing to the non-Communist reader.

RELATION BETWEEN ALIENATION AND OTHER CONCEPTS

It should be clear by now that Brecht's notions of structure, staging, and acting are all related to the concept of alienation. It is essentially by means of structure, staging, and acting that alienation is effected; it is for the purpose of alienation that Brechtian structure, staging, and acting are what they are.

END

In his early theoretical writings, Brecht insisted on a **didactic** end for theater; theater should teach the audience that a better world is both necessary and possible. Later, he modified his position and argued that the proper end of theater, as of all art, is delight. Yet the delight proper to our scientific age is not the sort of delight one takes in eating candy, but the more profound delight that comes from discovering new truths about oneself and the world one lives in. In pleading the cause of delight, then, Brecht did not discard his earlier didacticism. Rather, he succeeded in reconciling the demands of teaching and of pleasing.

AUDIENCE

The theater of illusion demands of the audience a nonintellectual, emotional response based primarily on empathy, the tendency to put oneself in the place of characters on the stage, to feel what they feel. Brecht's theater, while not ruling out emotion, demands a more critical and intellectual response. The audience should not indulge in empathy, but exercise critical judgment toward what it sees on the stage.

ADDITIONAL TERMS

A few of Brecht's other terms may require some clarification:

GESTUS

A key word in Brecht's dramatic theory is Gestus. It is, unfortunately, a word for which there is no exact English equivalent. As Brecht uses the word, it seems to cover the entire range of external expressions of social relationships. A Gestus, then, is a revelation of a relationship by a deed, word, and look.

ARISTOTELIAN AND NON-ARISTOTELIAN

These terms should present no great difficulty. Rightly or wrongly, Brecht associated the theater of illusion with Aristotle, the Greek philosopher whose *Poetics* is the most influential critical study of drama ever written. Hence, he often refers to this theater as "Aristotelian" and to his own, anti-illusionist theater as "non-Aristotelian."

CRITIQUE

Brecht's theories should by no means be accepted uncritically. He himself was constantly revising them throughout his career, and it would be ironic indeed if theories that ask the audience to remain at all times critically alert were to be passively accepted. We have already noted that the Communist implications of Brecht's theory derive rather from Brecht's political faith than from the logic of the theory. We might add that Brecht oversimplifies the nature of the "theater of illusion." Even in that theater, the illusion is never so complete as Brecht suggests. The audience never entirely forgets that it is in a theater, and is never completely convinced that what is on the stage is life itself. Finally, Brecht overstates the case for his own kind of theater when he insists, as he too often does in his early writing, that it is the only kind of theater that is right for our time. Still, in making us see the illusionist **conventions** in a new light, Brecht, like a true Brechtian, reminds us that these **conventions** are not inevitable, that they can be modified or even abandoned. This critical "alienation" is perhaps the greatest contribution of Brecht the theoretician.

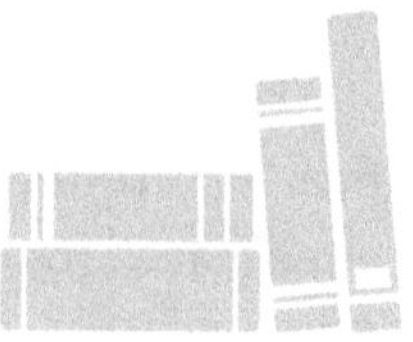

BAAL

INTRODUCTION

At one level, *Baal* was written in mockery of certain tendencies in the German theater in the early part of this century. At a more profound level, it is an expression of the nihilism that characterized the thought of Brecht in his pre-Communist days. (Nihilism: a denial of all values, of all abstractions by which man seeks to explain and justify his existence.) The denial of traditional values that is a subject of the play is reflected in Brecht's rejection of traditional dramatic form. He employs a loose, episodic structure, as if the tightly knit, artificial plot of the traditional form were incapable of containing the vitality of *Baal*, a vitality too great to accept the limitations of society and morality.

CHARACTERS

Baal: Poet, singer of songs in taverns, lover without prejudice of both women and men, ultimately an unrepentant murderer: in short, the hero of the play.

Mech: A publisher, among other things; a self-satisfied successful businessman.

Mrs. Mech (Emily): His wife, a beautiful and pliable young woman.

Dr. Piller: Critic, pedant, and literary politician.

Johannes Schmidt: A naive young admirer of Baal.

Johanna: Johannes Schmidt's innocent fiancee.

Ekart: Composer, companion to Baal, later his lover, ultimately his victim.

Louise: A waitress.

Two Sisters: Who share Baal's favors.

A Landlady

Sophie Barger: Another of Baal's women.

A Bum: Who blends liquor and religion.

Mjurk: The owner of a cafe where Baal is, for a time, employed.

Lupu, Chanteuse, Pianist: Employees of Mjurk.

A Parson: Who exposes one of Baal's schemes.

Bolleboll, Googoo, Maja, An Old Beggar: Derelicts at an inn.

A Young Woman: Mistress of Ekart, ravished by Baal.

Watzmann: A patron of a bar.

Bar Waitress

Two Rangers: Who pursue Baal.

Teamsters, Farmers, Lumberjacks, etc.

PROLOGUE

The prologue is a song about Baal. It celebrates the great energy of the hero and refers indirectly to the course of his life as it will be revealed in the play. The song also expresses Baal's amoral point of view: his refusal to recognize any meaning in the moral standards by which ordinary men are supposed to be bound.

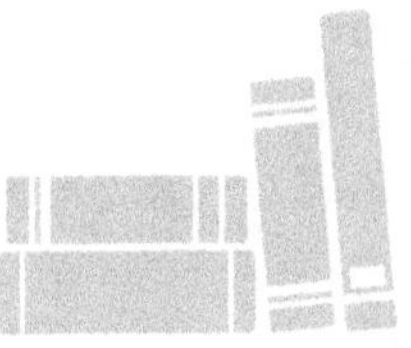

BAAL

SCENE SYNOPSES

SCENE ONE

Baal is among the dinner guests of Mech, the successful publisher, and his wife. Although it would be prudent for Baal to cultivate the patronage of Mech and the support of the influential critic Dr. Piller, who is also present, Baal is too taken with the attractions of Mech's wife Emily to notice. Finally outraged by Baal's behavior, Mech and Piller storm out of the room; the unconcerned Baal hurls a final insult at their departing backs. Young Johannes Schmidt, another dinner guest, expresses his admiration of Baal and asks Baal if he may visit him. Emily, although obviously fascinated, merely says that she is sorry for Baal. Finally left alone, Baal goes on drinking.

SCENE TWO

In the attic which is Baal's home Johannes tells Baal of Johanna, his beautiful and innocent sweetheart. Baal replies with brutal and cynical praise of purely physical love, but, recognizing that Johannes is not strong enough to abandon the support of conventional morality, Baal cautions the younger man against following his advice.

SCENE THREE

The setting is a bar room. Baal's complaint to some rowdy teamsters that Emily, with whom he has been having an affair, now won't leave him alone, is interrupted by the arrival of Johannes; with him is Johanna, his fiancee, whom he introduces to Baal. Soon Emily enters. She is forced to endure the insulting behavior of Baal, including his obvious flirtation with Johanna. Ekart, a composer, urges Baal to leave this foul dive. Baal is tempted to do so but resists the temptation, and Ekart leaves in disgust. Finally left alone with Emily, Baal seizes her brutally.

SCENE FOUR

This scene is divided into three parts, all of which take place in Baal's attic.

1. It is dawn. Johanna has spent the night with Baal. She feels deep remorse at what she has done. Receiving no sympathy from Baal, she leaves in despair.

2. It is noon. Two sisters arrive at Baal's attic. As they undress they tell Baal of a girl - Johanna, we discover - who has drowned herself. They are interrupted by the landlady, who, while expressing some sympathy for the misguided girls, forces them to leave for their own good and threatens the unconcerned Baal with eviction.

3. It is evening, several days later. Baal, who has spent the intervening time writing a poem, feels the need of a woman and goes out in search of one. After Baal leaves, Johannes enters. Upon his return with a young girl, Baal refuses to listen to Johannes' cries and makes him leave. The girl, Sophie, is frightened and hesitant, but finally unable to resist Baal.

Comment

The first scene is the only one in the play in which we see Baal in the context of a respectably bourgeois social occasion, and his behavior there indicates how little he belongs in such a context. These early scenes establish Baal's amorality, his refusal to accept the code by which others are bound. They also impress upon us the immense vitality of Baal, as we observe the hypnotic effect his personality has on characters like Johannes and Emily. The principal emphasis is on Baal's relations with women. They are his victims but, it seems, his willing victims. It is as if they want to be humiliated. With the introduction of Sophie, following the suicide of Johanna, we see the cycle beginning again.

It is significant that Johanna dies by drowning. Images of drowning, of floating helplessly down a stream and so on, occur frequently in this play and throughout Brecht's early dramatic work. This **imagery**, with its overtones of helplessness and aimlessness, may be seen as a reflection of the young Brecht's nihilism.

SCENE FIVE

In a street decorated to celebrate the feast of Corpus Christi, Baal enters into a religious dispute with a drunken bum. Disgusted, Baal steals the bum's bottle and departs.

SCENE SIX

Baal and Sophie are lying under some trees on a night in May. Sophie, who has remained with Baal since the night in April when he first took her his to room (**Scene Four**), now fears her mother must believe she is dead. Baal ignores her worries and begins to make love to her.

SCENE SEVEN

The setting is the dressing room of a cafe where Baal, now growing fatter, sits stripped to the waist, waiting to go on to sing his songs. He complains to Lupu, a fat young man who is sitting with him, that he has no brandy; it is in his contract that he will receive brandy in payment for his singing. When he goes on stage, Baal sings an obscene song that angers part of the audience and delights the rest. After coming off stage and arguing with Mjurk, the cafe owner, who has decreed that Baal may not have brandy before the performance, Baal escapes from the cafe by way of the window in the toilet.

Comment

Religious fanaticism disgusts Baal, because he feels that religious belief is associated with guilt and with the power of death over life. **Scene Seven** reintroduces the **theme** of the businessman's exploitation of the artist, which was first brought to our attention in **Scene One**. But Baal's situation has changed for the worse. He is growing fat. His exploiter is not the highly successful and powerful Mech, but the unsavory Mjurk, owner of a disreputable night spot. And Baal no longer dominates by the force of his personality, but must make an undignified escape. We begin to note some hints of mortality in this vital character.

SCENE EIGHT

Baal and Ekart are walking through green fields on a July day. Baal identifies himself with the forces of nature that surround him and Ekart.

SCENE NINE

The setting is a village tavern at evening. Baal has arranged an elaborate swindle of some farmers, encouraging them to bring their bulls to the village in the hope of selling them to Baal's brother, who does not exist. Ekart, who is with Baal, fears that the ruse will be discovered and that he and Baal will be severely punished, but Baal, happily drinking corn brandy, is unconcerned. A parson enters. He has seen through Baal's swindle and asks Baal why he has embarked on such a scheme. Baal replies that everything is a swindle anyway, and besides, the arrival of the bulls from seven villages and the farmer's gradual discovery that their greed has led them to be deceived will provide a wonderful show. The parson, a good-natured man, agrees not to punish Baal and Ekart and promises to pay for their drinks if they will simply leave.

Comment

The effect of these scenes is to make us see Baal as almost a force of nature, half-justifying his disdain for the morality by which mere men are bound. (Baal, of course, is the name of the ancient Near Eastern fertility god.) What looks like a swindle turns out be a huge practical joke, undertaken out of a desire to enjoy the spectacle. We sense that Baal feels remote from ordinary men, and we are aware of a curious innocence, perhaps the amoral innocence of nature itself, that distinguishes Baal from the greedy, but easily duped, farmers.

SCENE TEN

The setting is a lumber camp. Seven lumberjacks, one of them Baal, are sitting around the corpse of another lumberjack, named Teddy, who has apparently been killed in an accident. They talk about Teddy and incidentally revile Baal for his laziness. Baal makes a short speech over Teddy's body, in which and he says that the dead have rest, the living restlessness, and both are all right. One of the lumberjacks suggests that it would be fitting, in honor of Teddy, to drink up the brandy the dead man has left behind. Baal protests that it is disgraceful to steal a dead man's brandy, but it is discovered that Baal has already drunk it up. Baal justifies himself by saying that, while liquor does nothing for most men, it gives him great insights.

Comment

Coming about halfway through the play, this is a scene of the highest importance in the over-all design of the work. It foreshadows the last scene of the play, in which Baal is left alone to die by a group of lumberjacks. The speech over Teddy's body, in which Baal declares his acceptance of rest and restlessness, of life and death, is one of the play's most important statements. It suggests a change in Baal, who before seemed to reject death as vigorously as he asserted life. Baal the poet is developing into Baal the philosopher. At the same time, the scene is richly comic, as Baal, in berating the others for wanting to take Teddy's brandy, assumes the role of moralist - not a role in which we can take him seriously.

SCENE ELEVEN

Baal and Ekart in a cabin. Baal complains that he can't get rid of Sophie. Baal is growing fatter, Ekart thinner, approaching, as he puts it, a "mathematical condition." Sophie arrives and asks Baal for permission to come in.

SCENE TWELVE

Sophie, Baal, and Ekart on the plains at evening. Sophie insists she loves Baal in spite of everything. Ekart berates Baal for mistreating Sophie, who is now pregnant. Unrepentant, Baal tells Sophie to drown herself. Enraged, Ekart attacks Baal. They wrestle. What begins as a wrestling match develops into a sexual embrace. Baal drags the now unresisting Ekart away, leaving Sophie alone.

SCENE THIRTEEN

Baal and Ekart enter a room at an inn, in which they find Googoo, Bolleboll, the Beggar, and Maja, who has her child with her in a box.

The room is identified as the hospital tavern. All drink together, and Bolleboll tries to make love to Maja. Googoo makes a speech in which he declares that the most beautiful of all things is Nothing. Finally disgusted with the people and the surroundings, Baal and Ekart leave to wash themselves in the river.

SCENE FOURTEEN

Lying in a thicket, Baal tells Ekart that he has no further need of women.

SCENE FIFTEEN

Baal and Ekart in a field by a highway. Baal recites to Ekart a poem about a drowned girl. Ekart and Baal talk philosophy. Baal says the world is God's excrement; Ekart says God revealed His true nature in combining the sex organ and the urinary tract. Baal and Ekart then talk of a redhead to whom Ekart has been making love. Baal, jealous, asks if the girl is better looking than he is.

SCENE SIXTEEN

Baal alone in a field. Ekart's redhead appears. Ball threatens her, then takes her by force.

SCENE SEVENTEEN

Baal and Ekart seated at the foot of a tree. Baal recites to Ekart a poem called "Death in the Forest." Ekart hints he suspects what Baal has done to the redhead.

Comments

This section of the play reasserts several motifs that have been introduced earlier, as well as moving the action forward. The appearance of Sophie shows us again Baal's attitude towards women and is the occasion of another reference to death by drowning. Baal continues to grow fat. Baal's relationship with Ekart is, however, different from those he has had with women. Towards Ekart, Baal is possessive and jealous. His treatment of the redhead is obviously a punishment for Ekart's infidelity.

The philosophical exchange between Baal and Ekart (**Scene Fifteen**) and Googoo's speech in praise of Nothing (**Scene Thirteen**) restate the basic nihilism of the play.

In general, in this section, we find Baal less in control of his environment than before. His thoughts turn increasingly to the subject of death. The poem "Death in the Forest" foreshadows the death that awaits Baal himself; this is the second important **foreshadowing** of Baal's death. (See **Scene Ten**.)

SCENE EIGHTEEN

The setting is a barroom. Among those present are Baal, Ekart, Johannes Schmidt, a man named Watzmann, and a waitress who resembles Sophie. Johannes is drinking heavily; he is obsessed with memories of the drowned Johanna. When Watzmann turns up the lights, Baal sees that Ekart has the waitress sitting in his lap. Enraged, he throws himself on Ekart. In the ensuing struggle, Ekart is killed.

SCENE NINETEEN

In a forest, Baal is fleeing his pursuers. He sings a few snatches from the song of the prologue.

SCENE TWENTY

Hiding in some bushes, Baal overhears the conversation of two rangers who are pursuing him. It is from this conversation that he first learns that Ekart is indeed dead. Showing no remorse, Baal observes only that things are becoming interesting.

SCENE TWENTY-ONE

In a logger's cabin, Baal is dying. The loggers prepare to desert him, and one spits in his face, yet Baal laughs, because, he says, he likes the taste. Left alone, Baal finds the cabin stuffy. On all fours, he crawls outside to die beneath the stars.

Comment

In refusing to repent for killing Ekart, Baal defies to the end the demands of a moral code he refuses to recognize. Baal's death in the forest fulfills the prophecies implicit in Scenes Ten and Seventeen. His defiance gains him nothing tangible; he must die, like all men. Yet throughout the latter part of the play, as his fortunes descend and his actions become, if anything, more vicious than before, Baal develops a philosophical acceptance of things as they are. The categories of life and death, like those of good and evil, have become meaningless to him. Like a corpse floating down a stream, he no longer struggles against the flux that is the only reality.

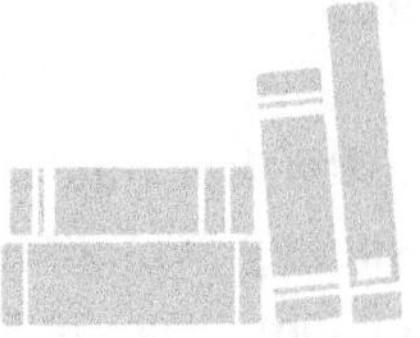

BAAL

CHARACTER ANALYSES

Baal

In a sense, Baal himself is the only fully developed character in the play. He is a figure of paradox. Guilty of behavior that ranges from the outrageous to the vicious, he yet retains a curious innocence. It is as though his refusal to acknowledge any sense of guilt were justified because guilt is human and Baal is something more than human - a force of nature, innocent because human morality does not apply to nature.

The women in *Baal* are all victims, but this seems to be the role they want to play. It may be argued that the limited view of women as interchangeable victims of male power is a weakness in the play.

Ekart

Ekart is the one character who seems at any time to have an upper hand over Baal. Something of ascetic, he may represent to Baal a spiritual intensity that Baal would like to share. Like Baal, he is rejected by society, which, in its reliance on narrow **convention**, seems to have little room for either the flesh or the spirit.

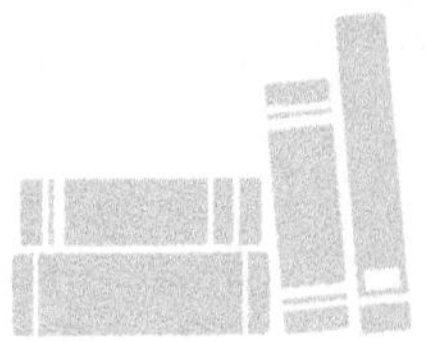

IN THE SWAMP (IM DICKICHT DER STAEDTE; IN THE JUNGLE OF CITIES)

INTRODUCTION

Even more eccentric in construction than *Baal, In the Swamp* (1921-24) is one of Brecht's most difficult works. It is almost certainly the most despairing play to come out of Brecht's nihilistic period, and one of the most powerful of his entire career. In a forward, Brecht warns us not to waste time trying to understand the motives of the characters, but to concentrate on the style of the contestants and to direct our attention to the finish. It may be worth noting that at this time of his life Brecht was fascinated with sporting events, spent much time in the company of prize fighters and other professional athletes, and in his critical writings, frequently pointed out relationships between sporting events and theatre.

SETTING

The announced setting of the play is Chicago, but the reader will quickly recognized that Brecht's Chicago is an imaginary city, a seaport from which it is possible to sail to Tahiti.

CHARACTERS

Shlink: A Malayan lumber dealer.

George Garga: At the outset, a clerk in a rental library.

John And Mae Garga: George's parents.

Marie Garga: George's sister.

Jane Larry: George's girlfriend.

Skinny: Shlink's secretary, a Chinese.

Collie Couch: Also known as Baboon, a pimp.

J. Finnay: Also known as Worm, a hotel owner.

Pat Mankyboddle: A coxswain, known familiarly as "Manky."

A Man From The Salvation Army

Snub Nose: Patron of a bar

Ken Si: Saloon keeper.

C. Maynes: Owner of a rental library.

A Waiter, A Male Secretary, An Employee, Various Men

IN THE SWAMP (IM DICKICHT DER STAEDTE; IN THE JUNGLE OF CITIES)

SCENE SYNOPSES

SCENE ONE

The setting is C. Maynes' Rental Library in Chicago on the morning of August 8, 1912. Shlink enters, accompanied by his secretary Skinny, and asks to buy George Garga's opinion of a mystery story. Garga agrees to sell the opinions of Mr. J. V. Jensen and Mr. Arthur Rimbaud, but insists his own opinions are not for sale. Although his family, which came from the plains, is poor and miserable in the city, Garga will not set a price on his own intelligence. C. Maynes, the owner of the library, enters, and Shlink complains that Garga is on strike. The Worm enters, knocks over some books, and walks over them. The Baboon enters with Jane Larry, whom he treats as a prostitute; she has spent the morning in bed with him. Shlink offers to double the price, but Garga refuses to sell. Maynes fires Garga. In a frenzy, Garga reads a passage from Rimbaud's *A Season in Hell*, tears off some of his clothes, and runs out. Shlink buys the clothes Garga has left behind from Maynes.

Comment

This is the first round of the fight that Shlink, for motives that are mysterious, wants to start with Garga. In offering to buy his opinions, Shlink outrages Garga's romantic idealism. It is obviously Shlink who has engineered the entire scene, including making a prostitute of Garga's girlfriend. The first round goes to Shlink.

Garga refers to J. V. Jensen and Arthur Rimbaud. Jensen, a Danish novelist, is the author of *The Wheel*, the action of which provided part of Brecht's inspiration for *In the Swamp*. Arthur Rimbaud, a French poet of the later nineteenth century, became involved in a homosexual relationship with another poet, Paul Verlaine. This relationship also seems to have been in Brecht's mind when he wrote *In the Swamp*.

SCENE TWO

The setting is Shlink's office on the evening of August 22. Garga enters. He has been drifting since being fired, but now he is ready to accept Shlink's challenge and fight, without asking for a reason. As soon as this is agreed upon, Shlink gives his house and lumber business to Garga, to make the fight more even. Garga immediately involves the lumber company in a fraudulent deal, making sure that Shlink will have to take the blame. He orders Skinny to pour ink over all the firm's records, then orders Shlink to fire Skinny. Shlink follows Garga's orders without demur. Garga's sister Marie has been employed by Shlink to take care of the laundry, and while Garga and Shlink are out of the room, Skinny, Worm, and Baboon discuss how much Marie's favors would be worth. A man from the Salvation Army enters. Garga agrees to give him Shlink's property, on condition that Shlink spit in the man's face. Shlink does so. Garga leaves, announcing he is going to Tahiti. Shlink leaves, followed by Marie.

Comment

Who has won round two? Shlink's tactic is passivity. Although he loses everything in the space of a few minutes, he is still in control of the fight. And, at the end of the round, he now has Marie.

SCENE THREE

John Garga, Mae Garga, and Manky are in the Garga's living room when George enters. George gives his mother enough money to last six months, then asks her to come to Tahiti with him. She refuses, but agrees to get his things ready. When they have left the room, the Worm enters. He complains to Manky and George's parents that Marie is lowering the moral tone of his Chinese hotel and asks that George be sent to get her. The Worm sneaks out when he notices Shlink standing in the doorway. Shlink presents himself to the Gargas as a poor man, and they agree to take him in.

Comment

By an ironic twist, Shlink replaces George in the Garga family. Note that Shlink, while seeming hardly to assert himself, remains in control of the fight; he has forced George into the role of aggressor. Shlink is like the boxer who, in the terminology of the sports pages, makes his opponent come to him. Note too, as an insight into Brecht's strategy, that he emphasizes the difference between the styles of Shlink and of Garga, granting us no hint of motives.

SCENE FOUR

The setting is the Chinese hotel. Both Jane and Marie are there. Shlink tells Marie of a disease from which he suffers; his skin has been abnormally thick since his youth on the rowboats of the Yangtze Kiang River, where he became accustomed to being tortured. Marie has fallen in love with Shlink, but Shlink is still obsessed with George. He is trying to locate the ship in which George intends to leave for Tahiti.

Comment

Thinness and thickness of skin are related here to a capacity for feeling. Human skin is by nature too thin for this world - that is, men's feelings are too easily touched, causing them pain. It is therefore necessary to thicken one's skin, as a form of protection. But the thickening process, once begun, cannot be halted, and the skin ultimately becomes so thick that one cannot feel at all. This, Shlink says, is what happened to him. We may wonder whether the same thing is not happening to George.

SCENE FIVE

The setting is the Chinese Hotel, about a month later. Visible are a dirty bedroom, a hallway, and a bar. George is in the bedroom. In the bar are the Worm, the Baboon, Jane, and Manky. Marie enters, and George unfeelingly berates her for what she has become. Shlink enters. He expresses his gratitude to George for not going to Tahiti. George indicates he is tired of this fight, but Shlink says George can't leave the ring innocent. George insists that Shlink and Marie make love, but Marie leaves with Manky, who says he loves her still. George demands that Shlink now give him the money made on a fraud perpetrated when Shlink gave George his lumber business. After taking the money from Shlink, George leaves with Jane. Shlink calls for rice and a chair, but the Worm and the Baboon tell him they won't support him any longer.

Comment

This richly ironic scene is of central importance in the play. Shlink's submissiveness is forcing George into increasingly aggressive actions. George is now willing to use Marie and Jane as mere objects in the struggle, at the same time that he insists he wants to end the fight. Shlink's submissiveness is therefore ironic, in that it is actually his most potent weapon. The fight is still following Shlink's plan. Yet there is a further **irony**. Shlink's submissiveness, however calculated, loses him the respect of the Worm and the Baboon. This is the first indication that the fight may be reaching a turning point.

SCENE SIX

Shlink and Marie are in a wood by Lake Michigan. Marie expresses disgust with her life as a prostitute and says she still loves Shlink. He is willing, as a matter of form, to say he loves her. They go into the bushes to make love. While they are gone, Manky appears, looking for Marie. He carries a gun and raves incoherently. After he leaves, Marie and Shlink return.

She insists that, as a whore, she should be paid for her services. Shlink pays her.

Comment

Marie observes after she and Shlink have made love that he treats her like a sacrifice. In a sense that is what she is; a sacrifice to the fight between Shlink and George. But by demanding payment, Marie compromises Shlink's submissiveness. She forces him into the role of willing customer. This is a further indication that the fight is no longer going Shlink's way.

SCENE SEVEN

George and Jane have just been married, and a wedding breakfast is being celebrated in the Gargas' living room. Besides George and Jane, those present are George's parents and Manky. In spite of the apparently festive occasion, George's mother observes that his mind is still on the fight with Shlink. Shlink arrives, carrying a letter revealing that the lumber fraud has been discovered; he waits for George's orders. After a moment's hesitation, George decides to take the blame and go to jail himself. Shlink is angered at this turn of events. George goes to call the police, and Shlink and Jane leave. George's mother, hinting to her husband that George has just been damned, goes out, saying that she is going to do something definite. Marie enters. Although he berates her for the life she is leading, her father accepts some money from her before she goes. George returns, having called the police. He writes a letter accusing Shlink of pursuing Jane and of seducing Marie. He plans to turn this letter over to the police just before being released from prison three years hence. He is sure that, because of Shlink's color, yellow, these accusations will assure that Shlink will be lynched.

Comment

George borrows Shlink's Style. George's willingness to submit to imprisonment leaves Shlink without a countermeasure, George's relation to Jane provides a pointed parallel to Shlink's relation to Marie. In fact, at this point George and Shlink seem to be becoming very much alike.

SCENE EIGHT

Shlink's office in the afternoon of October 20, 1915, about three years after George was sent to prison, Shlink, once more a successful businessman, dictates a letter refusing a job to Marie. A man arrives to tell Shlink that George's letter has arrived at the police commissioner's office. Shlink prepares to make an escape.

Comment

George has now clearly gained the upper hand; Shlink is losing the late rounds. The **irony** is that Shlink seems to have thought that, with George in prison, he was free of the fight.

SCENE NINE

The setting is a bar in the Chinese quarter on October 28, the day of George's release from prison. Present in the bar are the Worm, the Baboon, Jane, a man named Snub Nose, and the man from the Salvation Army. Their conversation reveals that a lynch mob is searching for Shlink, and in the orgy of lynching, no yellow man is safe. Marie sits by herself, throwing the money she has earned as a prostitute into a pail of water. George enters with C. Maynes and three other men, who are to serve as witnesses to the injustice George has suffered. George points out Jane and Marie to the men and tells them his mother has been missing for three years. They agree that George has suffered terrible injustices. George offers to forgive Jane her infidelities, but she leaves with the Baboon. George asks the Worm if he wasn't a former employee of Shlink, but the Worm denies he has ever known Shlink and scurries out. The man from the Salvation Army goes outside and tries to shoot himself but misses, suffering only a slight flesh wound. Maynes and the others carry him away, leaving Marie and George alone. Shlink is still the most important man in in their lives but George says he is finally free of Shlink. He has managed to finish Shlink without having to face him. He tells Marie to go home and wait for him. After Marie has gone, Shlink enters. The lynch mob is close behind him. He persuades George to come with him.

Comment

George is now clearly winning, but not entirely on his own terms. His offers of forgiveness are rejected by Jane, and, we discover, he is not really free of Shlink, after all. He must face his opponent one more time. Brecht introduced certain religious overtones in this scene. The nickelodeon plays "Ave Maria" right after the Worm has denied Shlink, as Peter denied Christ. The Salvation Army man's inability even to kill himself is an ironic image of man's impotence.

SCENE TEN

The setting is an abandoned tent along the gravel pits of Lake Michigan. Three weeks have passed. Shlink and George discuss the meaning of their fight. Shlink wanted to establish contact with another human through enmity. To struggle with another man, he hoped, would permit some kind of human contact, which is otherwise impossible. It was, then, the combat itself and not victory that he sought. He tells George he loves him. But George dismisses Shlink as unappetizing. Shlink wanted the combat; George wanted to win. Shlink fought for the sake of contact; George, for the sake of survival. Thus, George has won. Bored, he goes to betray Shlink to the lynch mob that is nearby. Marie enters and offers to help Shlink hide. But with the fight over, Shlink has no desire to run any longer. He drinks poison. When the lynchers arrive, Marie tells them Shlink is dead.

Comment

In the scene we realize the full force of the nihilistic despair on which the play is based. Shlink's hope is itself based on despair. If he wants to make contact through enmity, it is because he recognizes the impossibility of human contact on any other grounds. But Shlink's hope-born-of-despair proves as vain as any other, as he is forced to recognize that he has been unable to establish any real contact with George. Inescapable isolation is man's ultimate condition.

George's attitude is less romantic. From the idealist of the first scene, he has been transformed into the tough-minded realist, bent only on survival, victorious because he is younger and stronger. His skin has thickened.

SCENE ELEVEN

The scene is Shlink's office - now George's property-eight days after Shlink's death. George is present, along with his sister and father. George, who has decided to go to New York, wants to sell the burned-out lumber yard. Manky appears and offers to buy it. George agrees, on condition that Manky take Marie as part of the deal. Manky accepts this condition. The others go out, leaving George alone. He reflects on what has happened and concludes, "That was the best time."

Comment

What are we to make of George's final conclusion? Is it possible that the absurd combat in which he has been involved offered at least some hint of meaning in a universe otherwise meaningless? At any rate, George's final attitude towards his experience is nostalgia.

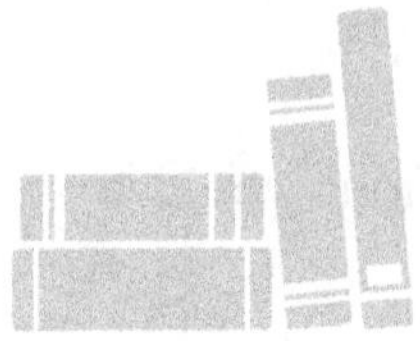

IN THE SWAMP (IM DICKICHT DER STAEDTE; IN THE JUNGLE OF CITIES)

CHARACTER ANALYSES

George Garga

When we first see him, George is a romantic idealist, unwilling to sell his intelligence at any price. By the end of the play, he is satisfied merely to survive, to continue his "naked life," as Shlink puts it. A naked life seems to be a life stripped of the kind of ideals George had formerly cherished. Now he feels that a naked life is the best kind of life. Forced into a fight he does not want or understand, George finally becomes an accomplished fighter indeed. But this involves a complete transformation of his personality. Brecht argued in his criticism that the notion of individual character as known, fixed, consistent - the notion that prevails in "Aristotelian" drama (see **Introduction**) - is an illusion. Man, he said in 1931, is a process. Thus, to understand George Garga is to understand not a "character" but a "process." He is completely transformed in the course of the play because external circumstances demand this process of transformation as a condition of survival. To object that George should have shown more "character," that he should have resisted the process of transformation, would be to misunderstand Brecht and his world.

Shlink

Although he is the original aggressor in the fight, Shlink's style, to which Brecht advises us to pay attention, is based on submissiveness. This style is not merely a matter of superficial technique. Shlink's submissiveness is related to his obvious masochism, his desire to suffer pain and humiliation.

Shlink's relation to George is obviously sexual - that is, homosexual - but, as Shlink himself points out, it is also; and perhaps more importantly, **metaphysical**. It is for what it reveals of the human condition, of the nature of this being we call man, that this relationship is significant.

One of the play's many ironies is that, at the end, it is Shlink who still reveals something of idealism. But it would be a mistake to assume that, because of this faint idealism, Shlink is being offered to us as some sort of model. In the world Brecht shows us in this play, the idealist has no place. It is right -that is, in keeping with things as they are - that Shlink should finally suffer defeat.

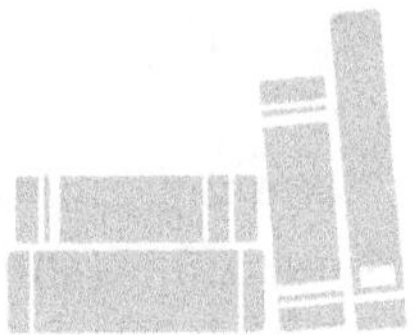

A MAN'S A MAN (MANN IST MANN; MAN IS MAN; MAN EQUALS MAN)

INTRODUCTION

The complete transformation of a human personality, that of George Garga, was one element of Brecht's *In the Swamp*. In *A Man's a Man* (1924-26), the transformation of personality becomes the central **theme**. Set in an India vaguely modeled on the stories of Rudyard Kipling and as unlike the real India as the Chicago of *In the Swamp* was unlike the real Chicago, *A Man's a Man* is one of Brecht' broadest and funniest plays. Yet its ultimate meaning is a matter of dispute. Is Brecht's **irony** at the expense of modern man, who has so slight a sense of identity? Or is the **irony** at the expense of the traditional humanist emphasis on the value of the individual personality? Perhaps Brecht, at this point in his career, is willing endorse Galy Gay's final conclusion that one's identity is not really worth making a great fuss over.

CHARACTERS

Galy Gay: An Irish packer who can't say "No." Another in Brecht's gallery of submissive characters.

Uriah Shelley, Jesse Mahoney, Polly Baker, Jeraiah Jip: Four members of a machine-gun unit (sometimes known as The Scum) in the British Army.

Mrs. Gay: Galy Gay's wife.

Charles Fairchild, alias Bloody Five: A sergeant who inspires terror in his men.

Mister Wang: Who runs a temple and knows a good thing when he sees one.

The Sexton: Of the temple.

Widow Leocadia Begbick: Owner of a canteen, provider of entertainment for the troops.

The Widow's Daughters: Part of the entertainment.

Jobia, Bessie, Ann, Soldiers

A MAN'S A MAN (MANN IST MANN; MAN IS MAN; MAN EQUALS MAN)

SCENE SYNOPSES

SCENE ONE

The setting is Kilkva, an imaginary city in India. Galy Gay decides to go out and buy a fish, in spite of his wife's warnings against lewd fishwives and brawling soldiers.

SCENE TWO

Uriah Shelley, Jesse Mahoney, Polly Baker, and Jeraiah Jip (sometimes known as The Scum) raid a temple to steal money for whiskey, but find the temple is full of traps. They manage to escape, but one of them, Jeraiah Jip, has lost a patch of hair. Fearing that his bald patch will make Jip easy to identify, the other three hide him in a leather chest. They plan to return after dark and shave Jip's head clean.

SCENE THREE

A road between Kilkva and the British camp. The three Scum-Uriah, Jesse, and Polly - are accosted by Bloody Five. He is looking for four soldiers, one of whom has a bald patch. The three Scum realize they will have to find someone to take Jip's place at roll call. At this point Galy Gay passes, following Widow Begbick, whose basket of cucumbers he carriers. Hours have passed since Galy left home. The widow tries to seduce Galy, but he doesn't seem to understand what she has in mind. The three soldiers decide that Galy Gay is a simple man who cannot say "No." They persuade him to accompany them to the Widow's canteen.

SCENE FOUR

Uriah, Jesse, and Polly buy a uniform from the Widow and dress Galy Gay in it. They are afraid that it will rain. If it does, the chest in which Jip is hidden will be carried inside the temple and they will not be able to get at Jip. As the widow Begbick knows, the rain will also mean another complication. Rain always arouses the sensual desires of Bloody Five.

SCENE FIVE

Meanwhile back at the temple, Mister Wang finds the drunk and confused Jip in the chest. Wang decides to put Jip on display as a god, since having a god around is always good in the temple business. Jip's three comrades come looking for him, but Wang frightens them off by threatening to see that they are arrested for trying to rob his temple.

SCENE SIX

Back at the canteen, the three soldiers fear that Jip won't be coming back. But since this is too depressing to think about they decide to go to sleep.

SCENE SEVEN

The temple again. Jip wants to leave, but Wang placates him by serving him steak. Wang doesn't want to lose Jip, who has been a great success as a god.

SCENE EIGHT

The canteen. Galy Gay is becoming worried, but Uriah, Jesse, and Polly persuade him to stay by offering to include him in a lucrative business deal. Bloody Five turns up with Galy Gay's wife, but Galy won't admit his true identity, and finally even Mrs. Gay is no longer sure that this is her husband. After Bloody Five and Mrs. Gay leave, the three soldiers decide that Galy must be transformed into Jeraiah Jip. This should be easy, since they have Jip's identity card, and an identity card is more important than a man.

SCENE NINE

In an elaborate scene divided into "numbers" introduced by Uriah, the transformation of Galy Gay is completed. Galy sells the Widow an artificial elephant in the belief that it is a real one. As a result of this transaction he is accused of fraud, placed on trial, and sentenced to be shot. The sight of the rifles pointed at him makes him faint. When he comes to, he is told Galy Gay has been shot and is asked to deliver a funeral oration. By this time he is no longer sure who he is, but he delivers the oration as requested. The soldiers, including Galy, who now carries Jip's identity card, set off for the war in Tibet.

SCENE TEN

On the way to Tibet, Bloody Five, fearing that the sensuality aroused in him by rainy days threatens his identity, castrates himself. Galy Gay thinks this is too much fuss to make over a name and is now quite willing to believe he's Jip, having seen what can come of stubbornness in such matters.

SCENE ELEVEN

Tibet. Jip finally turns up, but the others give him Galy Gay's identification card and send him away. They have created their own Jip out of the former Galy Gay and have no need of another. Galy Gay, transformed into Jip, has become the most ferocious soldier of all. He forces the others to give him their rations and wins the battle single-handed. Uriah, Jesse, and Polly are left wondering just what they have created.

Comment

In *A Man's a Man* Brecht reveals a comic spirit that may not have been obvious in such earlier works as *Baal* and *In the Swamp*. Yet a closer look at these earlier works will confirm the presence in them of a strain of dark comedy. By the same token, *A Man's a Man* picks up certain **themes** that have already established themselves as central in his work. We have noted in the introduction that the transformation of personality, a **theme** we saw in *In the Swamp*, is present here as well. Also, in Galy Gay Brecht depicts a character who is spiritually related to Shlink in his submissiveness and in the perverse delight he seems to take in his humiliations. Brecht's generally unsympathetic portrayal of Widow Begbick is consistent with the generally negative attitude toward women that prevails in Brecht's early work. For students of Brecht, however, the Widow Begbick may be most interesting as a kind of crude early sketch for one of Brecht's greatest creations: Mother Courage.

The play's most noteworthy structural element is the ironic parallel drawn between Galy Gay and Bloody Five. For Bloody Five the sense of identity is so important that, when he feels it threatened, he castrates himself. For Galy Gay identity is less important that survival. This recalls the conclusion reached by George Garga at the end of *In the Swamp*.

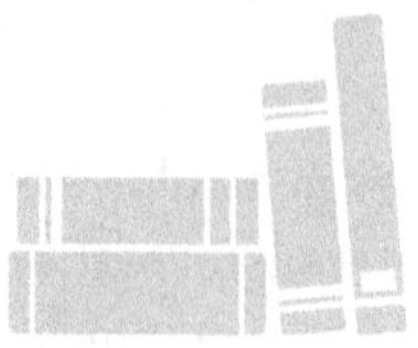

THE THREEPENNY OPERA (DIE DREIGROSCHENOPER)

INTRODUCTION

The Threepenny Opera, which has proven to be Brecht's most popular work, is based on the eighteenth-century English comic work, *The Beggar's Opera*, by John Gay. Gay wrote his play to satirize the aristocracy of the time by pointing out similarities between them and the rogues who made up his list of characters. Brecht's strategy is similar, but his target is the middle-class. It seems, however, that the German middle-class audience who made *The Threepenny Opera* a great popular success were not aware that they were its targets. Brecht suffered the especially ironic fate that seems reserved for ironists: his **irony** went unnoticed. Certainly, the modern audience of *The Threepenny Opera* should also notice those elements in the play that disguised its ironic intentions.

The music for *The Threepenny Opera* was composed by Kurt Weill, with whom Brecht collaborated on several other works, notably *Aufstieg und Fall der Stadt Mahagonny* (*Rise and Fall of the Town of Mahagonny*, 1928-29).

CHARACTERS

Captain Macheath (Mack The Knife): Murderer, thief, pimp, seducer of women, close friend of the Sheriff of London.

Jonathan Jeremiah Peachum: Owner of the firm called "The Beggar's Friend." His control over the beggars makes him one of the most powerful men in London.

Mrs. Celia Peachum: His wife and helpmate.

Polly Peachum: Their not entirely devoted daughter; later the wife of Macheath.

Ginny Jenny: A prostitute; occasional mistress and former business associate of Macheath.

Charles Filch: Whose ambition is to be a successful beggar.

John Brown (Tiger Brown): The Sheriff of London and a faithful friend as long as there's a profit in it.

Lucy Brown: His daughter, one of Mack's conquests.

Macheath's gang: Money Matthew, Crookfinger Jacob, Robert (Buzz The Saw), Ed, Jimmy The Second, Walter (Wally The Weeper)

Whores: Diana, Vixen, Dolly, Betty, Old Trull, Coaxer, Molly

The Reverend Kimball: A friend of Macheath.

Beggars, Constables, And A Street Singer

PROLOGUE

Setting

A fairground in Soho, a section of London. A street singer sings a "Moritat," celebrating the many crimes of Captain Macheath, alias Mack the Knife.

Comment

A Moritat is a kind of **ballad**, consisting of a narrative poem in quatrains (**stanzas** of four lines) set to a simple melody. The Moritat is often illustrated by a set of pictures to which the singer points as he sings. Because of its many popular arrangements, this particular Moritat is probably the work by which Brecht is best known to American audiences; of course, many Americans who whistle the Moritat have never heard of Brecht. The song, with its detached attitude (insisted upon by Weill's music) toward theft, rape, and multiple murder, sets the tone for the play to follow. We are not to be permitted the luxury of moral outrage.

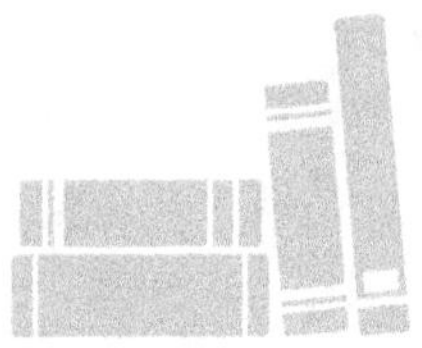

THE THREEPENNY OPERA (DIE DREIGROSCHENOPER)

TEXTUAL ANALYSIS

ACT ONE

SCENE ONE

The setting is Peachum's establishment for beggars. After singing his morning hymn, Peachum complains about the increasing difficulty of arousing pity. New gimmicks must always be found, and there is always the danger that eventually the gimmicks will be all used up. At this point Filch enters. This young man has been foolhardy enough to set himself up as a beggar without Peachum's approval. Peachum's functions are to issue licenses to beggars, to assign them to locations, and to provide them with such equipment as crutches, artificial limbs, fake sores, and the like. He is also a talented dramatic coach, skilled at demonstrating how to play a blind man, a cripple, or a sensitive young lad who has seen better days. In return for these services, Peachum receives from fifty to seventy per cent of the money the beggars take in. No beggar may work in London without a license from Peachum. Properly intimidated, Filch accepts Peachum's terms and sets out to strive and succeed in the begging profession.

Although Peachum's business is thriving, all is not well in the Peachum household. His daughter, Polly, who could be useful to him in the business, is instead seeing some man without her father's permission. The outraged parent questions his wife. From her description of Polly's young man, it becomes clear to Peachum that this is none other than the notorious Captain Macheath, otherwise known as Mack the Knife. To add to their worries, the Peachum's discover that Polly is not in her room. They sing a song expressing their concern.

Comment

We are of course prepared to laugh at Peachum's businesslike operation of his establishment for beggars. Certainly it is funny to see methods of respectable business enterprise applied to so disreputable an activity as begging. But this is not all there is to it. If begging is so profitable a venture that Peachum can thrive on it, this suggests that more respectable forms of enterprise are not doing a very good job of providing for the populace. Moreover, does Peachum differ so much from any businessman who makes a profit out of other men's endeavors? Finally, Peachum's job would be less difficult is only it were not so hard to arouse human pity among the middle classes on whom the beggars depend for subsistence. In short, the joke is only superficially on Peachum.

Peachum also echoes middle-class sentiments in his concern that his daughter will become involved with the wrong kind of man. To be sure, the average middle-class father is not prepared, as Peachum seems to be, to turn his daughter into a whore for the sake of business. The average father simply wants his daughter to marry well - that is, profitably.

SCENE TWO

The setting is an empty stable where Mack and Polly have come to be married. Polly is disturbed at the thought of being married in a stable, but soon the members of Mack's gang arrive, bearing furniture and other objects they have stolen for the occasion. Mack is appalled at the lack of taste revealed in their choices and complains that he is surrounded by men who have no sense of style. He orders them to dress in clothes suitable for a wedding. they select proper attire from among the stolen goods.

The festivities continue. Matthew, one of the gang, makes an off-color remark to Polly. Although she does not object, Mack is out-raged to hear this sort of talk in front of his bride. An outright fight is averted, however, and all sit down to a meal, made up of items stolen from some of London's best restaurants. During the meal Mack is disturbed when members of the gang make references to his many love affairs. Besides, the gang's table manners are atrocious. Finally, the Reverend Kimball arrives to perform the ceremony. Some of the gang sing a song as entertainment, and Polly, in her turn, sings the Song of Pirate Jenny, a celebration of suppressed violence which she once heard a barmaid sing in Soho.

At this point the gang is alarmed to note the arrival of Tiger Brown, the Sheriff of London. But Brown turns out to be a boyhood friend of Mack, and their friendship has continued to the present day. They sing a song of reminiscence of their days together in the army. Their conversation makes clear that their friendship has been profitable for both. Brown receives a generous share of the profits from Mack's activities and, in turn, warns Mack of police raids and makes sure that no charges against Mack go into the files at Scotland Yard. In a general air of good feeling, the guests depart, leaving Mack and Polly alone with the stolen bed to enjoy the bliss of their wedding night.

Comment

This scene becomes most effective when one sees it against the background of the conventional middle-class wedding- which is, after all, what Mack and Polly are aiming for. Mack's values especially are, apart from the peculiar nature of his profession, entirely of the middle class. He is much concerned with appearances: the style of furniture, the appropriateness of dress, the propriety of language, the correctness of table manners. The friendship of Mack and Brown, based firmly on practical interests, may be seen as a barbed comment on middle-class customs.

SCENE THREE

Polly has returned home to gather her things. Inevitably, she quarrels with her parents about what she has done. In a song, she explains that, while she could always say "No" to a gentlemen, she was unable to resist the crude Macheath. The argument is interrupted by the arrival of five beggars, complaining of the inferior equipment Peachum has given them. Peachum deals with them and returns to the argument with Polly. She insists that, although Mack is not handsome, he is a good provider; after a few more jobs, they'll be able to retire to the country. But Peachum is adamant. He demands that Polly get a divorce. Polly refuses to think of it. In the course of the argument, a new idea takes shape in Peachum's mind: perhaps he could arrange to have Macheath hanged. Besides ridding him of an unwanted son-in-law, this plan might even mean a modest reward. There would be no difficulty in finding Macheath, for Mrs. Peachum is sure he will be with his whores. The scene ends with a cynical song sung by the Peachum family.

Comment

In this scene the basic action of the plot begins to develop, as Peachum becomes aware of the possibilities of having Macheath hanged. At the same time the comedy at the expense of middle-class values continues. Polly sounds exactly like a sensible daughter of the middle class as she points out her husband's solid virtues as a provider. Peachum's willingness to see Macheath hanged may suggest that there is no honor among thieves. The question is whether there is honor among anybody.

THE THREEPENNY OPERA (DIE DREIGROSCHENOPER)

TEXTUAL ANALYSIS

ACT TWO

SCENE ONE

Polly comes to the stable to warn Mack that he is in danger. Under pressure from her father the reluctant Tiger Brown has agreed to arrest Mack. What is worse, Brown has inserted a full record of Mack's many crimes in the files of Scotland Yard. Mack decides that he should indeed make a hasty departure and tells Polly he will leave her in charge of the business. He shows her the account books and explains how to run the operation. In fact, Mack is not overly disturbed at this turn in his fortunes, since he plans soon to leave burglary and enter the banking profession anyway. Banking, he points out, is a safer and more profitable business. As part of his plan, he intends, when the time is right, to double cross his entire gang.

Members of the gang arrive, and Mack tells them they will be taking orders from Polly for the time being. The idea of taking orders from a woman is not pleasing to the gang. The coronation of the Queen is about to take place and will provide unusual opportunities for theft. Will Polly be able to handle the unexpected rush of business? Mack assures them of Polly's capability. This settled, Mack turns to criticizing Matthew, one of the gang, for trying to take the credit for setting fire to a children's hospital. Mack feels the credit is rightfully his. Having thus arranged his business affairs, Mack says a sentimental farewell to Polly.

Comment

Further reflections on honor are encouraged as we see Tiger Brown prepared to betray his old friend Mackie. But we are allowed no time to develop any sympathy for Macheath, surrounded as he is by betrayal, for we are soon made aware of Mack's willingness to betray his gang.

That the play takes place against the background of a coronation, that symbolic pageant of imperial majesty, is of course no accident. Brecht invites us to look at some parts of the Empire that are not included in the rituals of royalty. From this perspective, the Coronation seems rather less impressive than it might to a wide-eyed tourist.

Mack's ambition to go into banking is another comment on the life of the middle class. Mack recognizes no moral distinction between burglary and banking; the latter is merely safer and more profitable. Is Brecht guilty here of an outrageous distortion of reality? As this comment is being written, in the Spring of 1965, the United States Senate is engaged in investigating the extent of underworld influence in the operations of American banks.

INTERLUDE

Mrs. Peachum tells Ginny Jenny, one of Mack's many mistresses, to turn him over to the police and offers her a reward often shillings. Jenny is afraid that Mack will be hiding out, but Mrs. Peachum points out that men are creatures of habit. In a song, Jenny and Mrs. Peachum reflect on the nature of men, all of whom are helpless victims of their own sexual desires.

Comment

The view of men expressed in the song sung in this interlude is implicit in much of Brecht's early work. Man is unable rationally to serve his own interests because he is the victim of forces, both internal and external, that he does not understand. Jenny's willingness to turn in her old lower widens the circle of betrayal that Brecht is drawing for us.

SCENE TWO

Although he is being pursued by the police, Mack pays a visit to his whores at Wapping. It is Thursday, he always visits his whores on Thursday, and he refuses to change his habits for the sake of trifles. Among the girls present is Ginny Jenny, who reads Mack's palm. What she finds there is not encouraging, but Mack refuses to be discouraged. He chats with the girls and doesn't notice when Jenny steps outside. Moved to something like nostalgia, Mack sings a song in which he reminisces about his good old days with Jenny, when they lived together and she supported the two of them with her earnings as a prostitute. Jenny returns and joins Mack in the song. When they finish singing, a police constable enters to arrest Mack. He attempts to escape through the window but finds Mrs. Peachum and two other constables waiting for him. He is led off to Old Bailey, the London prison.

Comment

As Mrs. Peachum had predicted, Macheath is trapped by sex, although he may not see it that way.

SCENE THREE

Nervously waiting at Old Bailey, Tiger Brown hopes his old friend and business associate, Mack the Knife, will not be caught. When he sees Mack led in, he is conscience stricken. Unable to bear Macheath's scorn, Brown leaves. By bribing one of the constables, Macheath is able to avoid wearing handcuffs. In his cell he sings a song, the moral of which seems to be that money - and only money - can bring happiness. Lucy Brown, the Sheriff's daughter, enters and berates Mack for mistreating her. Her appearance and comments indicate she is pregnant by him. While Mack is trying to soothe Lucy, Polly enters. She and Lucy immediately begin insulting each other and express their jealousy and mutual dislike in a duet. Mack is embarrassed by Polly's presence, since he knows Lucy can help him. Fortunately for him, Mrs. Peachum arrives and takes Polly away.

Left alone with Lucy, Macheath manages to placate her and, with her assistance, escapes from the prison. Tiger Brown discovers that Mack has escaped and is delighted until Peachum arrives to claim his reward. Angered at Mack's escape, Peachum threatens to ruin Brown's career by using the beggars to cause an uproar at the coronation. Brown realizes he must recapture Mack the knife.

As a finale to **Act Two**, Macheath and Jenny sing a song which points out that man's livelihood depends on those acts we are accustomed to call mortal sins. "Eats first, morals later."

Comment

The encounter of Lucy and Polly, arousing Macheath's discomfiture, provides one of the plays most amusing comic moments, and their duet, now raucous, now sentimental, is a musical delight. This seems as good a point as any to suggest the importance of becoming familiar with the music to which Weill set Brecht's lyrics.

Tiger Brown's difficulties in this scene point up one of Brecht's characteristic ideas; that being wicked is hard work. Mack's discomfiture before Lucy and Polly may point the same moral. The song that ends **Act Two** expresses a familiar Brechtian **theme**, one that runs through this play. Morality is a luxury that can be enjoyed only by those who do not have to struggle for economic necessities.

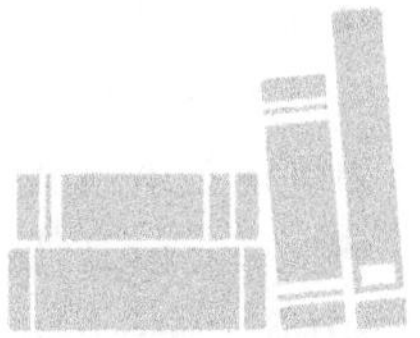

THE THREEPENNY OPERA (DIE DREIGROSCHENOPER)

TEXTUAL ANALYSIS

ACT THREE

SCENE ONE

At his establishment, Peachum and some of his beggars are making posters in preparation for the riot that is to take place at the coronation parade. Ginny Jenny and the other girls come to collect the promised reward, but the Peachums refuse to pay because Macheath has escaped. In the angry outburst that follows, Jenny reveals that Mackie, having paid her a visit, is now in the arms of Suky Tawdry, another of his whores. Convinced that this information assures the apprehension of Macheath, Mrs. Peachum tells Jenny to come back for her money after the coronation.

Led by Tiger Brown, the police arrive. Brown intends to arrest Peachum and the others who are there and threatens to make short work of any beggars who show up at the parade. Unperturbed, Peachum points out that the sight of police cracking beggars' heads at the coronation parade would hardly be an edifying one for the Queen and the respectable onlookers. He then tells the crestfallen Brown where Macheath may be found.

Comment

Once again, Macheath's sensuality is his downfall. And once again, Brown is helpless in the face of the power complex represented by Peachum and his beggars. This situation may be seen as a **metaphor** for the relation between the agencies of the state and the economic interests that often exercise control over these agencies. A few years after Brecht wrote this play, a film version, directed by G. W. Pabst, was made in Germany. The film draws an explicit parallel between the actions of the Peachum's beggars and the latent power of the downtrodden. In the play itself, however, written before Brecht's commitment to communism, this revolutionary point in not insisted upon.

INTERLUDE

Ginny Jenny sings a song which claims it is men's virtues that bring them to grief.

SCENE TWO

Polly visits Lucy Brown. As if embarrassed by their earlier encounter, both ladies make a careful show of good manners. In reality, Polly is hoping to learn of Mack's whereabouts, but Lucy doesn't know. One thing that is revealed by their conversation is that Lucy is not really pregnant, but only pretended to be for

Mack's sake. Mrs. Peachum arrives, carrying widow's weeds for Polly to put on. Mack has been captured again; this time he will surely hang.

Comment

Much of the comic point of this scene is in the **parody** of middle-class manners that we observe in the behavior of Polly and Lucy. Brecht sharply observes the forced politeness of people who detest each other.

Note that the second capture of Macheath occurs offstage. The circumstances of the capture repeat those of the first capture, thus restating Brecht's comic point that men are creatures of habit, especially that they are unable to resist the lure of sexual satisfaction. They are prisoners of forces they do not understand. Yet in making this point, Brecht does not want to be guilty of anti-climactic repetition in his dramatic structure. He avoids this fault by presenting this second capture indirectly. This also allows him to concentrate on the effect of Mack's capture on the ladies.

SCENE THREE

The death cell. Macheath's hanging is expected to be a great attraction. In fact, there is some fear that so many people will attend the hanging that no one will be at the coronation. Macheath, however, has no desire to be the star attraction under these circumstances. Having satisfied himself that the constable guarding him can be bribed, Macheath resolves to raise the thousand pounds necessary before the hour set for the hanging.

Two members of Mack's gang, Matthew and Jacob, visit Mack and grudgingly agree to bring him all they have - four hundred pounds - if they can get through the crowds that are gathering. Polly also visits Mack, but she can't help him because she has sent their money to Southampton. At this point almost all the characters of the play arrive for Macheath's hanging. Matthew and Jacob return without the money; they have been unable to get through the crowds. They also bring apologies from other gang members, who would like to be with Mack in his final hour, but who, as industrious thieves, cannot pass up the opportunities for theft presented by the coronation. Mack understands. It is difficult for the independent artisan to survive against the competition of large concerns backed by banks. Mack sings a farewell song, in which he ironically forgives all who have done him wrong. He is now ready to be hanged.

But a happy ending is in store. Just as Macheath is to be hanged, Tiger Brown appears in the role of a Royal Messenger. Macheath has been pardoned! But that is not all. The Queen has raised him to the nobility and given him a castle and pension for the rest of his life. All step to the front of the stage and sing a final hymn.

Comment

As the Peachums observe, happy endings are very nice in the theater, but in reality Royal Messengers arrive all too seldom. At any rate, the happy ending allows Mack to realize the dream of the middle-class man: to be raised to the nobility.

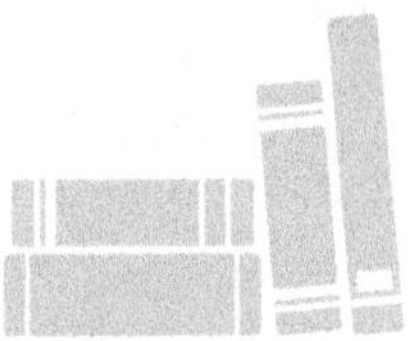

THE THREEPENNY OPERA (DIE DREIGROSCHENOPER)

CHARACTER ANALYSES

Macheath

The key to Macheath's character is that he is thoroughly bourgeois. He should not be visualized as a dashing romantic hero; Polly tells us that he is not handsome. He probably looks rather like a shopkeeper or traveling salesman. He is not immoral. Like Baal, he is amoral. He simply does not recognize that morality has anything to do with his action. To him, burning down a children's hospital is simply a rather impressive achievement. His relation to women is rather more complex than that of the characters in Brecht's earlier plays. In the earlier plays women were the victims of men. But Mackie is the victim of his own sensuality (rather like Bloody Five in *A Man's a Man*) and thus permits women to get the upper hand.

Peachum

Mr. Peachum is the strongest character in the play. Not only is he free of sentimentality himself, but he understands sentimentality in others. This understanding is the source of his success in business. The other characters in the play are all to some extent at the mercy of their feelings. Only Peachum is the fully conscious manipulator of feelings. Thus he can play on the feelings of others while remaining entirely detached himself. This is the source of his strength.

Polly Peachum

Polly is significantly different from the completely victimized women of Brecht's earlier plays. True, she is foolish enough to fall in love with the unfaithful Mackie. But she is also her father's daughter and proves capable of taking care of herself. She has no trouble asserting her authority over Macheath's gang, and, when it looks as though her Mackie is really going to be hanged, she prudently salts their money away in a safe place. What makes Polly different from the women of *Baal* and *In the Swamp* is that, however sentimental she may be on occasion, she understands the art of survival.

ST. JOAN OF THE STOCKYARDS (DIE HEILIGE JOHANNA DER SCHLACHTHOEFE)

INTRODUCTION

As its title suggests, *St. Joan of the Stockyards* is in part based on the life and legend of St. Joan of Arc, who helped liberate France in the fifteenth century. But in the play this raw material acquires a characteristically Brechtian twist. The setting is Brecht's mythical Chicago, and the play takes a newly serious look at a **theme** suggested in *The Threepenny Opera:* "Eats first, morals later." Among the play's stylistic devices are parodies of Shakespeare and of the German writers, Goethe and Schiller. Brecht seems also to have been influenced by the modern Irish playwright George Bernard Shaw, who had already written his own Saint Joan. The play by Shaw that seems most closely related to *St. Joan of the Stockyards* is not, however, Saint Joan, but *Major Barbara*, the study of a Salvation Army girl who is forced to face the realities of life.

CHARACTERS

Joan Dark: A member of the Black Straw Hats, a religious group obviously modeled on the Salvation Army.

Other Black Straw Hats: Martha, Major Paulus Snyder, Jackson

Tycoons of the meat industry: Pierpont Mauler, Cridle, Lennox, Graham, Slift

Mulberry: A landlord.

Mrs. Luckerniddle: Widow of a worker killed in an industrial accident.

Gloomb: A worker.

Mrs. Swingburn: A worker's wife.

A Waiter

An Old Man

A Broker

An Apprentice

Two Detectives

Five Labor Leaders

Two Policemen

And a number of minor characters who appear only as members of groups.

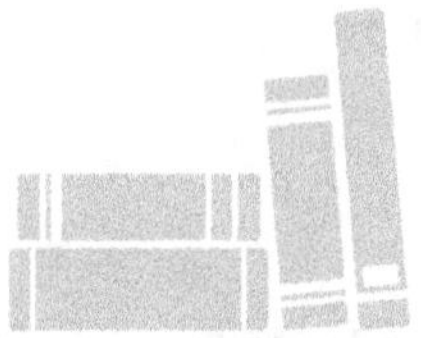

ST. JOAN OF THE STOCKYARDS (DIE HEILIGE JOHANNA DER SCHLACHTHOEFE)

SCENE SYNOPSES

SCENE ONE

The setting is the Chicago stockyards. The stock market is in trouble and Pierpont Mauler, the meat baron, has developed squeamishness at the sight of slaughtered animals and wants to leave the business completely. He persuades his associate, Cridle, to buy out his interest. A condition of the deal is that Mauler agrees to bring about the fall of Lennox, one of their rivals in the meat business.

Comment

Mauler is revealed as a paradoxical mixture of sentimentality and ruthlessness. Unable to bear the sight of an animal being slaughtered, he is yet willing to bring about the ruin of another human being.

SCENE TWO

In front of the Lennox plant, the workers protest against the low wages they receive for their labors. Newsboys run by, announcing that Lennox has been forced to close down the plant. The workers know that, while this may be an economic setback for Lennox, they are the ones who will really suffer.

A group of Black Straw Hats come along, singing a rousing marching song. Their aim is to re-introduce God in a world that seems to deny Him. It is not this world that matters, they say, but the next. One of them, Joan Dark, denounces the use of force to settle conflicts. The workers, however, are an unresponsive audience. They are more interested in jobs than in God. Moved by the sight of this misery, Joan wants to know who is responsible for it. The other Black Straw Hats warn her not to get involved in worldly quarrels, but she insists she wants to know.

Comment

The scene underlines the irrelevance of promises of the next world to men who are starving in this one. Joan's healthy curiosity, her desire to know, distinguishes her from her companions, who dismiss the real problems of the workers as "worldly." Joan's denunciation of force represents a moral position from which she will gradually be converted in the course of the play.

SCENES THREE AND FOUR

In her search for knowledge, Joan encounters Mauler. He is strangely impressed by her and wants her approval, but he considers her unrealistic. The poor, he argues, don't deserve sympathy, because they are wicked. Joan still insists she wants to know. Mauler arranges to have Slift, another tycoon, take Joan among the workers. On this guided tour Joan sees the poor behaving wickedly, but she realizes it is their poverty that makes them wicked. They are forced to do almost anything for money because they must struggle for survival.

Comment

As in *The Threepenny Opera*, but here with greater seriousness of tone, Brecht suggests that morality is a luxury to be enjoyed only by those who have economic security. Joan's ability to see this is an important step in her education.

SCENE FIVE

Mauler's activities have thrown the market into a panic. Breeders, packers, wholesalers all fear that they are on the verge of ruin, but Mauler sits by unconcerned. As the others revile Mauler, the sound of drums is heard. The Black Hats are coming, with Joan Dark at their head and an army of poor at their rear. Alarmed by the presence of the poor, Mauler feels obliged to buy from the packers, thus saving the market from collapse.

Comment

Joan is learning. Whether consciously or not, she senses that Mauler can carry on his shady practices only so long as he can avoid the sight of those who suffer from them. She is, then, using force, albeit moral rather than physical force, to gain her ends.

SCENE SIX

At his home, Mauler shows signs of having been affected by the sight of the poor. Slift points out that Mauler's deal with the packers will probably ruin him, but what worries Mauler is that he didn't act from how motives. What has gotten into him? Still, without knowing what he was doing, he may have made a good deal. A number of Congressmen having been bribed, tariff's are about to be lowered. Perhaps this was the time to buy, after all. But Mauler is alarmed to discover that Joan is outside. This time she is followed by the stock breeders, who want Mauler to buy their livestock. After some rapid figuring, Mauler agrees.

Comment

Mauler's terror at the realization that he has not acted from low motives suggests a typically Brechtian **theme**: the evil man is constantly being tempted to do good. For Brecht, then, evil is unnatural. A man must force himself to be evil and work hard at it, as Tiger Brown discovers in *The Threepenny Opera*. What this suggests is that Brecht's superficial cynicism masks an ultimate optimism.

SCENE SEVEN

The setting is the Mission of the Black Straw Hats. Snyder, the major of the Black Straw Hats, is trying to get the meat packers to support his mission, but they have problems of their own. Because all the livestock has been bought up, they cannot fulfill the terms of their contract with Mauler. Still, Snyder's offer is attractive. What he preaches to the starving workers, he points out, is that unhappiness is not caused by people (like their employers, for example) but falls like rain. If only the packers will support his mission - to the tune of eight hundred dollars a month - this inspiring message can continue.

This kind of talk reveals to Joan how much the rich use religion to stifle resistance among the poor. Enraged, she drives the packers from the mission. But her action in turn enrages the more sophisticated Major Snyder. Her orders Joan to leave.

Comment

Joan's action is clearly intended to remind us of Christ's driving the money changers from the temple. And Joan, like Christ, is misunderstood and mistreated.

SCENE EIGHT

Joan visits Mauler at his home. When she tells him of her misfortunes, he is moved to tears. He offers to give her money to take to the Black Straw Hats, to allow them to pay the rent to the grasping Mr. Mulberry, their landlord. He points out in a song that capitalism and religion depend on each other for support. Joan, however, refuses to accept Mauler's money. She prefers to stand with the poor, who have gathered in the stockyards to demand their rights.

Comment

That the main function of religion is to prevent the deprived from acting to improve their lot is a cherished Marxist belief. As Mauler's song indicates, Brecht by this time is pretty thoroughly committed to communism. But his critique of religion remains relevant for non-Communists as well. Note that Brecht does not attack the Christ who drove the money changers from the temple. It is the "Christians" who serve the interests of the money changers that he despises.

SCENE NINE

Joan has joined the poor in their struggle. She is with them when the Black Straw Hats arrive to preach the glories of the next world; but the poor are still unresponsive to this message. One of the workers says that only the Communists have any enterprise.

The scene shifts to the Livestock Exchange, where Mauler now offers to sell to the packers the stock that will allow them to fulfill their contract - but at his price. In the stockyards, a labor leader gives Joan a letter to deliver to three men from the Cridle plant.

At the Livestock Exchange, Mauler, assisted by Slift, forces the prices of stock higher and higher. Mauler also arranges to have the police attack the strikers who have gathered in the stockyards. In the stockyards, Joan is recognized by some reporters who think she is still with the Black Straw Hats. She tells them that capitalism is a seesaw. The few who are kept aloft at one end - the capitalists - owe their position to the collective weight of the many - the poor - at the other end. As Joan waits to deliver her message, the workers insist more and more vehemently that force is necessary. Joan realizes she will not be able to deliver the message entrusted to her, for she still cannot bring herself to take part in violence.

Comment

From Brecht's point of view, Joan's education is not yet complete. She still indulges in a self-righteousness that has nothing to do with the real and pressing needs of the poor. But her comparison of capitalism to a seesaw indicates that she understands things more clearly than she used to.

SCENE TEN

Prices have taken an unexpected drop, and Mauler is ruined. Rather pleased by this turn of events, Mauler presents himself at the Black Straw Hats' Mission as a sinner seeking salvation. The Black Straw Hats are not entirely pleased. Mauler is offering them his soul, but they had been hoping for a share of his money. All is not lost, however. Mauler's departure has left the market in a state of chaos, and the packers and other tycoons arrive to beg him to return and save them all. He agrees after some hesitation. He also agrees to see to the support of the mission, provided the Black Straw Hats continue to preach their message, which is so useful to businessmen like himself.

In the stockyards Joan witnesses the failure of the general strike. Conscious of her own failure to do her part in the strike, she falls to the ground.

SCENE ELEVEN

Dying, Joan is carried into the mission. Her last words indicate that at last she realizes that force is necessary if the poor are ever to be relieved of their suffering. But Mauler, the tycoons, and the Black Straw Hats ignore what she says. They prepare to spread the word that Joan was a saint, a martyr to the ideals of the Black Straw Hats.

Comment

At the moment of her death, Joan finally completes her education. The **irony** is that the others deny her death its true meaning by treating her as a martyr to ideals she no longer believed in.

ST. JOAN OF THE STOCKYARDS (DIE HEILIGE JOHANNA DER SCHLACHTHOEFE)

CHARACTER ANALYSES

Joan Dark

In her uncompromising search for truth, Joan is a heroic figure. She is transformed in the course of the play from a dedicated religionist to a dedicated revolutionary as she comes to realize that it is not immorality but poverty that must be fought. Yet her old beliefs die hard and it is her tragedy that she must contribute to the failure of the general strike before she realizes her error. Her courage and integrity clearly set her apart from the female characters in Brecht's earlier plays. In fact, from this point in his career, Brecht begins to paint a more positive picture of women.

Pierpont Mauler

Brecht's conception of the American capitalist is, of course, as fantastic - and as poetically convincing - as his conception of Chicago,. Mauler feels a constant temptation towards good, which he manages to resist only by a heroic struggle. He is helped in his struggle by the nature of the capitalist system, which allows him to remain detached from the evil consequences of his activities. When Joan forces him to look upon the poor victims of his shady practices, he weakens. Yet he is willing to strike them indirectly, through his market manipulations and through the agency of the police.

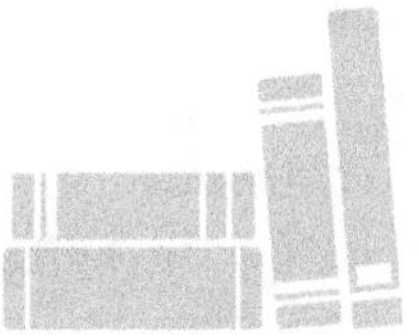

THE MEASURES TAKEN (DIE MASSNAHME; THE EXPEDIENT; THE DECISION)

SUMMARY

INTRODUCTION

In one sense this **didactic** work is Brecht's most thoroughly Communistic play, for its message is that the Communist discipline must be accepted without question. Yet the play has frequently been attacked by Communist critics, who feel that Brecht has portrayed this discipline as uncomfortably harsh. At any rate, this short, intense play is one of Brecht's most disturbing works. Some have argued that it is the only Marxist tragedy ever written.

SUMMARY

Four Communist agitators have killed a comrade because he wished the right thing and did the wrong thing. They have come to the Control Chorus to demand a verdict on the rightness or wrongness of the measures they have taken. The Chorus agrees to hear their story and to render a verdict. In the trial that follows, all parts are played by the agitators themselves.

THE AGITATOR'S STORY

Sent on a mission of propaganda and agitation to China, the agitators are welcomed just before they cross the frontier by a young comrade who expresses the hope that they have come to help him. Instead of offering help, the agitators demand an automobile and a guide. The young comrade obediently provides them with an automobile and offers himself as a guide. Before setting out, the agitators and their comrade, don masks: they must be willing to sacrifice their identities for the cause. Their present purpose, say the agitators, is not to abolish poverty but to make the poor recognize the cause of their poverty.

As the agitators attempt to carry out their mission, they are constantly frustrated by the young comrade, who makes the mistake of acting out of humane impulses rather than sticking to the job at hand. For example, when the police kill a worker, the young comrade leads an attack on the police. But the attack does not bring the dead man back to life, and the only practical result is that the agitators are unable to hand out the leaflets they were sent to distribute.

Finally, the young comrade becomes involved in an imprudent plan for an immediate revolution. He sees injustice and is unwilling to wait to bring it to an end. Although the agitators know the rebellion is really a plot by the merchants, they cannot argue the young comrade out of the foolish course he has chosen. The rebellion is, of course, a failure, and the young comrade makes the mistake of unmasking himself. The agitators strike him down and carry him away.

The young comrade has seriously endangered the mission. As long as he is with them, the agitators may easily be discovered. They decide they must kill the young comrade and throw his body in a lime pit to prevent identification. They tell their decision to the young comrade, who agrees that it is just and necessary. They shoot him and throw his body in the lime pit.

Rendering its verdict, the Control Chorus approves of the measures taken.

Comment

Brecht mistrusts the old-fashioned humanistic idea of personal identity as much as ever. But he has replaced the nihilism of his earlier plays with a new philosophy. *The Measures Taken* calls for absolute submission to the authority of the Communist party. It seems that communism provided Brecht with a principle of order he had been unable to find elsewhere.

For all its obviously **didactic** nature, *The Measures Taken* is truly dramatic. Brecht's ideas are embodied in a significant conflict, a conflict not between right and wrong, but between right and right. The young comrade is a brave and honorable man, but his patchwork reforms, even if successful, could only have the effect of delaying the ultimate awakening of the masses.

MOTHER COURAGE (MUTTER COURAGE UND IHRE KINDER)

INTRODUCTION

MOTHER COURAGE AND HER CHILDREN

One of Brecht's most admired plays, *Mother Courage* is set in Europe during the Thirty Years' War (1618-48), which was fought primarily between the Protestants and Catholics of the Holy Roman Empire. As might be expected, however, Brecht is only slightly concerned with historical accuracy, and the Thirty Years' War serves for him as a symbol of all war. The Thirty Years' War has, incidentally, special meaning for a German, since Germany suffered especially from its effects.

Like *St. Joan of the Stockyards* and *The Measures Taken, Mother Courage* is **didactic** in intention, but dramatic in fact. Audiences have persisted in regarding Mother Courage with more sympathy than they are supposed to, thus missing the full impact of Brecht's intended message. Whether it fulfills Brecht's intentions or not, *Mother Courage* is unquestionably a masterpiece. This may be the case in which the artist has, to use the American philosopher-poet Emerson's phrase, "builded better than he knew."

CHARACTERS

Anna Fierling, Or Mother Courage: A peddler who finds that business is good in wartime.

Eilif: Her brave son.

Swiss Cheese: Her honest son.

Kattrin: Her kind daughter.

Cook: Who has an interesting love life.

Chaplain: Who, out of necessity, travels with Mother Courage.

Yvette Poitier: A whore who makes good.

A number Of Unnamed Soldiers, Officers, Peasants, Etc.

The Time: 1624-36.

The Place: Sweden, Poland, Germany.

PROLOGUE

The wagon of *Mother Courage* appears. Seated on it are Mother Courage and her daughter Kattrin. The wagon is pulled by Mother Courage's sons Eilif and Swiss Cheese. As Kattrin plays a harmonica, the others sing "The Song of Mother Courage," a kind of singing commercial aimed at stirring up buyers for the wares Mother Courage has to sell. The message of the song, is, roughly, "Eat and drink today, you'll be dead tomorrow."

Comment

The song, of course, indicates the extent to which Mother Courage depends on war, with its constant threat of disaster, in her business. Yet the scene also suggests a kind of beatitude. The vital, singing family we are introduced to is be become victimized by the war on which their prosperity is based.

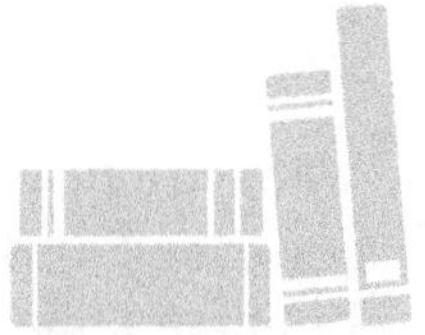

MOTHER COURAGE (MUTTER COURAGE UND IHRE KINDER)

SCENE SYNOPSES

SCENE ONE

In the year 1624, a sergeant and recruiting officer stand on a highway outside a town, looking for recruits for the Polish campaign planned by Gustavus of Sweden, a Protestant King. The wagon of Mother Courage approaches, and the two soldiers are quick to notice that she has two young sons of the right age for military service. For her part, Mother Courage sees the soldiers as prospective customers and willingly stops her wagon. She and the soldiers become engaged in a conversation in which it is revealed that Mother Courage's real name is Anna Fierling. She has been known as Mother Courage since she drove through the bombardment of Riga with fifty loaves of bread in her wagon. She couldn't afford to stop, because the bread was going moldy, she explains. She also mentioned that her three children have three different fathers and makes clear that she has enjoyed a varied love life.

All the while, the soldiers are primarily interested in getting at least one of Mother Courage's sons to enlist. They have their eyes especially on Eilif, who, in truth, longs for the life of a soldier. Mother Courage, however, has different ideas: no son of hers is going to get himself killed looking for military glory. To distract Mother Courage's attention, the sergeant expresses an interest in buying a new belt. While she is engaged in haggling over the price, the recruiting officer sneaks off with Eilif.

Comment

The play begins in 1624; by this time the Thirty Years' War has been underway for six years. Up to now, the war has been, for Mother Courage, primarily a situation that is good for business. But now a price is to be exacted: she must give a son to the war from which she has accepted prosperity. Mother Courage's character is vividly presented in this first scene. We recognize the **irony** in the anecdote of how she got her name; her thoughts were not on courage but on business. But we also recognize in the anecdote an instance of a remarkable endurance and vitality, an ability to go on in spite of adverse circumstances. A similar quality is suggested in Mother Courage's account of the origins of her children. Lovers come and lovers go, but Mother Courage endures.

Note that Mother Courage loses Eilif because she is distracted by business dealings as he is being led away. This will not be the last time that Mother Courage will be forced to regret her eagerness for a good deal.

Each of Mother Courage's children has one outstanding trait of character. In Swiss Cheese, who is not very bright, it is honesty. In Kattrin, who cannot speak, it is kindness. In Eilif, it is bravery, which makes him a natural choice for the army.

SCENE TWO

The time is about two years after the end of **Scene One**. Mother Courage has been following the Swedish Army through Poland. We find her in the kitchen of the Swedish Commander's tent, haggling with the Cook over the price of a capon. Their argument is interrupted by the Swedish Commander and two others. One is a Chaplain. The second is Eilif. He is enjoying the honor of being the Commander's personal guest as a reward for having slaughtered some peasants and stolen their bullocks. At the Commander's request, he sings a song. Mother Courage recognizes the voice and, seeing it is her son, joins in the song. Eilif is delighted to see his mother, and we learn that they have not met since Eilif enlisted two years before. Mother Courage is angry with Eilif - not for stealing the bullocks but for risking his neck by not surrendering to the peasants at once.

Comment

The nature of Eilif's heroic act reflects Brecht's attitude towards military glory: it is based on officially sanctioned murder and pillage. Mother Courage's attitude is also clear enough: don't stick your neck out.

SCENE THREE

It is three years later. Swiss Cheese has for some time been Paymaster of the Second Protestant Regiment. As the scene opens, Mother Courage, not without haggling, is buying some bullets from an ordinance officer. The deal closed, the officer goes off with Swiss Cheese. Mother Courage is joined by the Chaplain and the Cook, to whom she serves brandy.

At this point the sound of shots announces an attack by the Catholics. The Cook runs off to join the Regiment. Swiss Cheese returns, carrying the regimental cash box. Worried at being entrusted with the Regiment's funds, Swiss Cheese goes in search of a safe place to hide the cash box, but he is captured by soldiers of the Catholic Army.

Mother Courage, meanwhile, has run up the Catholic flag behind her wagon. When questioned about Swiss Cheese she pretends not to know him, saying he merely bought his lunch from her.

With the help of Yvette, a cooperative whore, Mother Courage gets a colonel in the Catholic Army to offer two hundred guilders for her wagon. With this two hundred, Yvette is to bribe one of the Catholic soldiers to let Swiss Cheese escape. But when Mother Courage hears that Swiss Cheese has thrown the cash box into the river, she decides she cannot afford the use the whole two hundred for the bribe; she must keep something to live on. She instructs Yvette to offer only one hundred and twenty. Yvette returns shortly and says the soldier won't accept the offer. Moreover, the roll of drums signifying a verdict is due any minute. Mother Courage says she'll pay the two hundred. But at this moment the roll of drums is heard. She has haggled too long.

Next morning some of the Catholic soldiers, intending to trap Mother Courage, bring Swiss Cheese's dead body to her. But she denies she knows him. The Catholic sergeant orders his men to throw Swiss Cheese's body on the garbage dump.

Comment

Mother Courage wants to save her son, but she takes money too seriously to offer a bigger bribe than necessary. After all, it looks as though she is going to lose her wagon, and she has Kattrin to think of. This is the second time Mother Courage has lost a son as a result of haggling. Whatever her good qualities, she does not learn from experience.

SCENE FOUR

Mother Courage arrives at a Catholic officer's tent to complain that some soldiers have damaged her wagon. While she is waiting to be admitted, an angry young soldier arrives. He too, wants to see the officer, whom he calls a thief. Mother Courage tries to calm the soldier down, pointing out that people who make noises only get into trouble. She sings a song in which she says that, sooner or later, everyone capitulates. Her arguments seems to persuade the soldier, who leaves. What is more, Mother Courage has persuaded herself. She decides not to complain, after all.

Comment

Mother Courage's is the negative wisdom of the person who survives by giving in. In this respect, she another of Brecht's submissive characters (see **analyses** of *In the Swamp* and *A Man's a Man*).

This scene provides a comic interlude after the tragedy of the preceding. Mother Courage's denial of her son's body and her decision not to complain are both based on the same instinct for survival.

SCENE FIVE

The setting is a war ravaged village near Leipzig in 1631. The Chaplain, who has been traveling with Mother Courage ever since he was cut off from the Protestant Regiment two years before (**Scene Three**), is tending to the wounded. Mother Courage is selling schnapps. One soldier complains that he can't afford any because he arrived too late for plunder. The Chaplain needs linen to make bandages with, but Mother Courage refuses to let him tear up the fine officer's shirts she is planning to sell. Kattrin threatens to spank her selfish mother with a stick, and the Chaplain takes the shirts by force.

From a ruined house that is ready to cave in, the cry of a baby is heard. Kattrin runs into the house, and the Chaplain is afraid to go in after her. In a moment, Kattrin returns, carrying the baby, to whom she hums a lullaby.

Comment

By showing us Mother Courage carrying on business as usual amid the wreckage caused by war, Brecht seeks to offset some of the sympathy we may feel for her. Although she loves her children, s e is always a tough and selfish woman.

Kattrin's rescue of the baby, underlining her kindness and especially her love for children, foreshadows her later heroic actions. It also provides a contrast to her mother's selfishness.

SCENE SIX

The year is 1632, and the place is a canteen tent near the city of Ingolstadt. General Tilly of the Catholic Army has been accidentally killed, and his soldiers, instead of honoring their general by attending his funeral, are getting drunk. Mother Courage is wondering how long the war will last. The Chaplain thinks it may never end. Thus assured that business will continue to be good, Mother Courage decides to stock up on supplies.

Noticing that Mother Courage has kept the pipe the Cook left behind when he ran off to join the Regiment (**Scene Three**), the Chaplain warns her that the Cook is a man of low character. The Chaplain also suggests he would like his relationship with Mother Courage to become more intimate. Before anything much can come of this, Kattrin enters. She has been attacked by soldiers, and her face is badly scarred. Mother Courage curses the war that has done this to her daughter.

Comment

If Mother Courage were capable of learning from experience, what happens to Kattrin would convince her of the evil and folly of trying to make a profit out of war. Yet her characteristic attitude remains that suggested earlier in the scene: war is good for business.

SCENE SEVEN

The setting is a highway. Mother Courage's wagon appears, pulled by Kattrin and the Chaplain, with Mother Courage walking alongside. The wagon itself is dirty and neglected, but new goods are hung from it. Mother Courage sings a chorus from "The Song of Mother Courage" (see **Prologue**).

Comment

Structurally, this short scene is an echo of the Prologue, and we recognize from the condition of the wagon and the absence of Eilif and Swiss Cheese how far we have come from the beatitude represented there.

The shock of her daughter's rape having worn off, it is once again business as usual for Mother Courage. She has learned nothing from her experience.

SCENE EIGHT

The death of the Swedish King has brought peace Having stocked up on supplies in the expectation of a long war, Mother Courage doesn't know what is to become of her.

The Cook turns up. He is overjoyed at the arrival of peace, but not pleased to see the Chaplain, whom he regards as a meddling windbag. The Chaplain once again dons his military uniform and prepares to rejoin the army. Angered at Mother Courage's grumbling that peace will ruin her business, the Chaplain calls her a hyena. Angry in her turn, Mother Courage accepts the Cook's advice that she rid herself of her wares before the price drops to zero.

Before Mother Courage can leave for the market, her old friend Yvette (**Scene Three**) enters. Yvette is now the wealthy widow of one of the Catholic colonels. She embarrasses the

Cook by recognizing him as the man who first seduced her, when she was still a young girl. She and the Cook argue, but Mother Courage persuades Yvette to come to the market with her.

While Mother Courage is gone, Eilif is led in by two soldiers. He is going to be executed for killing and robbing a peasant after peace was declared. The Chaplain and the Cook decide not to tell Mother Courage, who returns soon after, announcing that war has broken out again. Back in business, she sets out with her wagon, taking the Cook with her. She still doesn't know what has happened to Eilif.

Comment

This is one of the most richly ironic scenes in the play. Mother Courage's total inability to learn from experience is underlined by her disappointment at what looks like the arrival of peace. The folly of the position, clear enough in itself, is made even clearer when we discover that her son Eilif has become a victim of the war on which she depends for a living. Eilif's fate has its own ironies. He is condemned to death for acts like those that made him a hero in wartime. Moreover, the "peace" during which he acted turns out to be only a short pause in a continuing war.

SCENE NINE

The time is the autumn of 1634. The weather is severe and business is bad. A letter informs the Cook that he has an opportunity to open an inn in Utrecht. He asks Mother Courage to come along, but he doesn't want Kattrin. Dumb and mentally retarded, she would only be a bother, and, besides, the guests wouldn't want to look at someone so horribly scarred. Kattrin overhears the conversation and prepares to sneak away, but her mother finds her. Leaving the Cook's belongings behind, Kattrin and Mother Courage set out together, harnessed to the wagon.

Comment

Mother Courage's family feeling remains her most powerful emotion. This lends pathos to the **irony** of her depending on the war that has already taken two of her children and, we are sure, will ultimately take the third. Note the importance of the wagon in the economy of the play. On the one hand, it symbolizes solidarity and endurance. On the other, it is the burden of Mother Courage and her family, the massive object to which they are harnessed. Seen in this light, the wagon becomes a symbol of Mother Courage's materialism, a destructive force.

SCENE TEN

Passing by a prosperous farmhouse, Mother Courage and Kattrin hear someone inside singing a song in praise of shelter. They listen a while, then move on.

SCENE ELEVEN

It is January of 1636. The wagon, now in a dilapidated condition, stands in front of a farmhouse near the Protestant town of Halle. A Catholic lieutenant and some soldiers enter and force two old peasants, their young son, and Kattrin to come out of the house. (Mother Courage, as we learn in the next scene, is away on business.) It turns out that the Catholics are planning to attack the town while the people are asleep. When one of the peasants mentions that there are children in the town, Kattrin becomes troubled. Unnoticed, she climbs to the roof of the farmhouse and, hoping to wake the town, starts beating a drum she has hidden under her dress. Trying to stop her, the soldiers promise they will spare her mother if she will come down. Kattrin continues to beat the drum. The lieutenant orders the young peasant to break up the wagon. Kattrin makes frightened, whimpering noises, but beats the drum more loudly. The old peasants want Kattrin to stop, for they are afraid of the possible consequences for themselves, but their son shouts to her to go on. The soldiers kill the young peasant. Kattrin begins to cry, but beats the drum still more loudly. Finally, the soldiers shoot Kattrin, but her last feeble drumbeats are drowned out by the sound of shooting. The town is awake and defending itself against the attack.

Comment

In spite of his theories of alienation and detachment, Brecht has written here one of the most powerfully emotional scenes in modern drama. This should remind us of the folly of regarding Brecht's plays as mere illustrations of his theories.

SCENE TWELVE

Mother Courage sits on the ground by Kattrin's dead body. Trying to convince herself that Kattrin may only be sleeping, Mother Courage sings her a lullaby. But the old peasants tell her once again that her daughter is dead. They remind her, too, that the soldiers are marching off. She'd better get going if she doesn't want to be left behind. Mother Courage, who still doesn't know that Eilif is dead, gives the peasants some money to cover the expenses of burying Kattrin. Then she hitches herself to her wagon. She finds she can pull it alone; there isn't much in it any more. She sets off after the soldiers, who march to battle singing "The Song of Mother Courage."

Comment

Once again, Mother Courage has lost a child while distracted by business. All she has left is the burden of her wagon, which she must pull alone. The end of the war is not in sight.

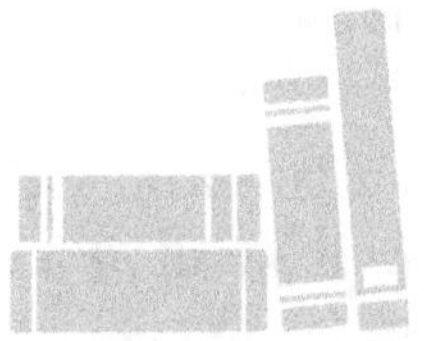

MOTHER COURAGE (MUTTER COURAGE UND IHRE KINDER)

CHARACTER ANALYSES

Mother Courage

As it was indicated in the introduction, Mother Courage seems to arouse in audiences a greater sympathy than Brecht desired. It is perhaps advisable, then, to remind ourselves first of her vices. She is, as the Chaplain says, a hyena, a scavenger. Her profits are based on the misery of others, and she shows little capacity for sympathy for anyone outside of her own family. The deaths of her children may all be traced, directly or indirectly, to her commercial instincts. It is her desire to make a profit out of the war that places them all in danger, and she is engaged in haggling of one sort or other when Eilif enlists, when Swiss Cheese is shot, when Eilif appears on his way to be executed, and when Kattrin is killed. Furthermore, she is incapable of self-knowledge or of learning from experience.

Yet we are moved by her fate. Perhaps it is because her grief is genuine, as is her love for her children. Or perhaps we sense something heroic in her tenacious struggle for survival, in her power of sheer endurance.

Perhaps, though, the answer is that we recognize how much of Mother Courage there is in all of us. If we cannot condemn her, it may be because we cannot condemn ourselves.

Kattrin

Kattrin is, throughout, a victim. Her dumbness is the result of her being abused by soldiers when a child. She is raped and disfigured, and the pathos of this is intensified as we learn that she longs to be married. Her most obvious trait is kindness, especially toward children, and it is this that motivates her final sacrifice. But note the skill with which Brecht avoids sentimentalizing her, for instance, by suggesting that she is capable of vanity and by such surprising evidences of vigor as her threat of beating Mother Courage in **Scene Five**.

Eilif

If Kattrin's dominant trait is kindness, Eilif's is bravery. Yet it is a bravery that smacks of foolhardiness and brutality. Eilif's "heroism" consists finally of murder and theft.

Swiss Cheese

Mother Courage brought Swiss Cheese up to be honest because he wasn't very bright. He isn't. His honesty is made to seem essentially a lack of imagination.

The Chaplain

The Chaplain is one of the most complex characters in the play. He is capable of cowardice, as when he salutes the Catholic flag to avoid being taken prisoner. Yet he is also capable of human feelings and actions, as when he cares for the wounded in **Scene Five**. He is given to philosophizing and is often pompous, yet there is sometimes more than a little wisdom in what he says.

The Cook

The Cook is a match for Mother Courage. He is thoroughly selfish and unscrupulous. Lacking the Chaplain's insight, he does not understand that Mother Courage will never desert her daughter.

GALILEO (LEBEN DES GALILEI)

INTRODUCTION

Galileo is based on historical fact. Galileo Galilei (1564-1642) was a great Italian physicist and astronomer whose investigations in the field of astronomy brought him to the attention of the Inquisition, a tribunal concerned with the judgment of heresies against the Catholic faith, and led ultimately to his being silenced by the Church.

The investigations that led to Galileo's difficulties resulted in the confirmation of the Copernican system of astronomy. For centuries, the Western world had accepted the so-called Ptolemaic system. According to the Ptolemaic system, the sun and other heavenly bodies revolve around the earth, which is the stable center of the universe. A few years before Galileo was born, a Polish astronomer called Nicolaus Kopernik, or Copernicus (1473-1543), had advanced the theory that the earth and other planets revolved around the sun; the earth was thus, as it were, removed from its privileged position at the center of the universe. This was the theory confirmed by the experiments of Galileo.

But why should the Inquisition, concerned with matters of religious faith, turn its attention to a matter so purely in the realm of science? The answer is that, rightly or wrongly, important scientific theories are often held to have philosophical, and even religious, implications. The Ptolemaic system placed the earth at the center of the universe; but at the center of the earth was man. Thus was revealed man's ultimate significance in the sight of God. Moreover, the Ptolemaic vision of an ordered, hierarchically structured universe provided, so it seemed, a cosmic basis for order and hierarchy in the Church and in society. Thus, the impact of Galileo's findings might be felt well beyond the narrow limits of the scientific realm. The Copernican system challenged man's conception of the universe he lived in, of the God he worshipped, and - what was perhaps most disturbing - of himself.

Although drawing his subject matter from these historical disputes, Brecht takes an artist's approach to his material. The character of his Galileo may bear little resemblance to the actual Italian scientist who died, a prisoner of the Inquisition, three centuries before Brecht wrote this play. In fact, many critics have seen in Brecht's **protagonist** a man similar in many ways to Brecht himself. In any event, the character of Galileo is one of Brecht's greatest triumphs and the play of which he is **protagonist** is surely one of Brecht's masterpieces.

CHARACTERS

Galileo Galilei: Physicist and astronomer; he hungers after knowledge.

Andrea Sarti: Galileo's pupil.

Mrs. Sarti: Galileo's housekeeper, Andrea's mother.

Virginia: Galileo's daughter.

Ludovico Marsili: A pupil of Galileo, later Virginia's fiance.

Matti: An iron founder, friendly to Galileo and to intellectual freedom.

Federzoni: An assistant to Galileo.

Little Monk: Who also assists Galileo and is torn between the faith demanded by the Church and the doubt proper to science.

Sagredo: A friend of Galileo.

Christopher Clavius: Chief Astronomer to the Papal College in Rome.

Cardinal Bellarmin: A learned and crafty churchman.

Cardinal Barberini: Churchman and mathematician, later Pope Urban VIII.

Priuli: A curator.

And a large number of minor characters, most of whom not identified by name.

GALILEO (LEBEN DES GALILEI)

SCENE SYNOPSES

SCENE ONE

The setting is the scantily furnished study of Galileo Galilei in Padua in the year 1609. Andrea Sarti, the son of Galileo's housekeeper, brings Galileo a gift from the Court of Naples. The gift is a map of the sky, drawn according to the conception of the Ptolemaic system (see **Introduction**). Galileo predicts that soon people will realize that, contrary to the Ptolemaic system, it is the earth that revolves around the sun. He demonstrates his meaning by having the washstand at which he was washing himself represent the sun. He then moves the chair in which Andrea sits to represent the earth. By this means, he demonstrates to Andrea that it is really the movement of the earth that makes it seem to us as though the sun were moving.

Mrs. Sarti brings Galileo his breakfast and complains that she doesn't approve of Galileo's filling her son's head with tales of the earth rolling around the sun. Galileo is disturbed to discover that Andre has spoken of his theory to Mrs. Sarti. He doesn't want his beliefs to come to the attention of the authorities.

A young man named Ludovico Marsili is announced. He wishes to become a pupil of Galileo. Galileo is not interested in taking on Marsili, who is obviously a far from brilliant prospect, but a look from Mrs. Sarti reminds Galileo that he needs the money this student will pay. What does interest Galileo is the young man's description of an instrument he has seen in Holland. We recognize from this description that Ludovico is talking of a telescope, but at this time no one outside of Holland had ever seen one. Ludovico leaves after Galileo accepts him as a student.

Priuli the curator, arrives, and Galileo immediately borrows from him a scudo, a coin of the period, and with it sends Andrea to buy him a pair of lenses. The curator has come to inform Galileo that his request for an honorarium has been denied. Galileo doesn't know how he will make ends meet. If he has to accept more students, this will leave him still less time for research. The curator suggests that Galileo might expect to be paid if only he will develop something practical. Galileo says he may do just that. The curator leaves, and Andrea returns with the lenses.

Comment

Brecht's Galileo is greedy for the satisfaction of both his body and his mind. An obstacle is that he must depend for his financial support on mediocre students or on the generosity of men who have no interest in science except as it serves some immediate practical end. Another is that he must take care that his unorthodox theories do not come to the attention of the political and ecclesiastical authorities who are inclined to equate the unorthodox in science with the unorthodox (and therefore potentially subversive) in politics and religion.

Somehow, Galileo must find ways to continue his work in this unfavorable environment.

Mrs. Sarti's bewilderment and resentment at the strange notions of her employer foreshadow the kind of difficulties Galileo will have to face as time goes on, while her son Andrea's intellectual curiosity suggests the role he will play in Galileo's life. Galileo's "demonstration" of the earth's revolutions to Andrea, through the example of the homely household furnishings, suggests Galileo's ability to use whatever is at hand, and is typical of Brechts' skillful use of stage properties to make dramatic points.

SCENE TWO

Before a group of dignitaries that includes senators, public officials, and the Doge himself, Galileo unveils his new, and eminently practical invention: the telescope. The dignitaries are much impressed at the power of this tube to make far-off objects appear very close; they see the value it might have in war, for instance. As a reward for his inventiveness, they are prepared to pay Galileo an additional five hundred scudi a year.

Galileo, meanwhile converses with his friend Sagredo. Galileo says he has been looking at the moon through his telescope and has found it doesn't give off its own light. He also tells Sagredo he now knows what the Milky Way is really made of.

Galileo's charming daughter Virginia brings an embarrassed Ludovico before Galileo. Galileo, on the defensive because Ludovico knows the telescope is not his invention, says "I improved it." Another member of the crowd is Matti, a prosperous iron founder from Florence. Matti is interested in a machine

Galileo designed for a foundry in Padua. Galileo promises to put Matti in touch with someone who will copy the design for him. Galileo himself doesn't expect to have time.

Comment

Galileo, we said in our Comment in **Scene One**, has the agility to make use of whatever is at hand. He has now made skillful if unscrupulous use of the information imparted by Ludovico Marsili. He has persuaded the unsuspecting citizens of the Republic of Venice that the telescope is his own invention. But note that Galileo is also making use of the telescope in his scientific investigations and that he is forced into his present deception by his need for money if he is to continue those investigations. He remains dedicated to science. He will not put himself at the service of Matti, although to do so would mean more money, because, having been promised additional funds, he wants to devote more time to his research.

SCENE THREE

In his study on the evening of January 10, 1610, Galileo is pointing out to Sagredo, who is looking through the telescope, the mountains on the moon. He tells Sagredo that the earth is a star. Sagredo replies that, if true, this gives the lie to two thousand years of astronomy.

This learned discussion is interrupted by the arrival of the angry Priuli. Galileo's fraud has been exposed, as Venice has been flooded with telescopes from Holland. Galileo is ruined in Venice. After the curator's departure, Galileo admits his deception to Sagredo, but insists that he needed the money.

What he really needs, indeed, is enough money to support five years of uninterrupted research.

After the interruption, Galileo and Sagredo continue their investigations with the telescope. Galileo shows his friend that the Milky Way is made up of stars. Hesitantly, Sagredo asks Galileo a question that has been troubling him. Yes, says Galileo, he does have some evidence that the earth revolves around the sun.

Galileo and Sagredo work through the night. They find that Jupiter has other stars revolving around it. Jupiter, then, is not attached to anything. There is no support in the heavens, says Galileo. Sagredo is frightened. Where then, he asks, is God? God, says Galileo, is within ourselves - or nowhere.

Virginia enters on her way to Mass. Galileo tells her they may be moving to Florence. He has sent the Florentine Prince Cosimo de Medici an obsequious letter seeking patronage. Although Galileo could live more comfortably in Florence, Sagredo has doubts about the wisdom of the plan. The monks are in power in Florence, he points out. He fears Galileo's insatiable search for truth will lead to trouble.

Comment

The comments and questions of Sagredo indicate the kind of philosophical and religious implications that will be seen in Galileo's discoveries. God cannot be located in this strange new universe that Galileo is exploring. We may well understand the cautious Sagredo's fear for his friend's safety in Florence.

Whatever curious investigations her father may be involved in, Virginia Galileo is as devout as she is charming. She gives not the slightest indication of understanding anything her father is doing, but responds to his commands with simple obedience. The idea of going to the splendid court of Florence pleases her.

SCENE FOUR

It seems that Galileo's flattering letter to Cosimo de Medici has served its purpose, for Galileo is now living in a well-appointed house in Florence - a definite contrast to his modest quarters in Padua. Galileo's guests at his house are a number of gentlemen and ladies of Cosimo de Medici's court, including a number of scholars, and the nine-year-old Prince Cosimo himself, who is looked after by the Lord Chamberlain. What Galileo intends is to demonstrate his telescope to Cosimo, but the young boy is rather tired and easily distracted, and the members of his court show little interest in Galileo's contraption. A philosopher expounds on the beauties of the universe, according to the Ptolemaic system. He expounds in Latin until Galileo insists that he speak in the vernacular; Galileo's new assistant, Federzoni, knows no Latin.

Galileo can get no one to look through his telescope. The philosopher says Galileo is trying to demonstrate the impossible, for what he claims can be seen through the telescope would contradict the writings of Aristotle on astronomy. A mathematician agrees that this is the last word. Finally, the sleepy Prince is led away. The Lord Chamberlain says that the Prince will seek the opinion of Christopher Clavius, Chief Astronomer to the Papal College in Rome.

Comment

The obstacles to learning that confound Galileo in this scene are several. First, there is simple indifference, which is pretty much the attitude of the courtiers. Then there is the feeling that learning should not be made easily accessible to the many, an attitude reflected in the philosopher's desire to speak in Latin, rather than in the vernacular, or native tongue of those present. Latin was at this time the language of learning. Finally, and most importantly, there is the reverence for authority that leads the philosopher to argue that what one can now see with one's own eyes (aided, of course, by the telescope) is impossible if it contradicts what the Greek philosopher Aristotle (who had no telescope) wrote almost two thousand years ago.

SCENE FIVE

The setting is a hall in the Collegium Romanum. In a room offstage the astronomer Clavius, using a telescope, is checking Galileo's observations about the movements of the heavenly bodies. Galileo sits by himself in a room full of prelates, monks, and scholars, none of whom believes there can be any truth in his claims. Most of them regard the theory that the earth revolves around the sun as merely funny. One old Cardinal, however, denounces Galileo as an enemy of mankind. The earth, says the Cardinal, is the center of all things, and man is the center of the earth. Now Galileo wants to deprive man of the exalted position granted him by God Himself.

Clavius emerges from the room in which he has been working and announces curtly that Galileo is right. A little monk approaches Galileo and says he overheard Clavius say that now the theologians must set the heaven right again.

Comment

The scene presents Galileo's greatest triumph to date, as the respected Clavius is forced to confirm his observations. Yet the outburst of the old Cardinal tells of the hostility Galileo must face. This kind of victory can be dangerous.

SCENE SIX

A party is in progress at the house in Rome of the learned Cardinal Bellarmin when Galileo arrives with his daughter Virginia and Ludovico Marsili, who has become her fiance. Virginia is dazzled by the crowd, which includes members of most of the great families of Italy. As she and Ludovico go to join the festivities, Galileo is joined by Cardinal Bellarmin and Cardinal Barberini, who is a brilliant mathematician as well as a powerful churchman. What seems to be good-natured badinage passes between Barberini and Galileo on the subject of the latter's theories. Each man quotes freely from the Bible, Barberini to attack Galileo's ideas and Galileo to defend them. The tone of the conversation changes when Bellarmin, instructing his secretaries to take down what is said from this point on, advises Galileo that the Holy Office (that is, the Inquisition) regards his theories as heresy. Still, the two churchmen seem to remain personally friendly as they invite Galileo to join them in returning to the party.

When the secretaries are left alone, we discover they have been taking down the entire conversation, even the informal and half-joking remarks that passed between Galileo and Barberini. The entrance at this point of the Cardinal Inquisitor reveals the intense interest the Holy Office is taking in Galileo. When Virginia passes by, the Cardinal Inquisitor engages her in conversation. Believing that this distinguished churchman is merely taking a friendly interest in her, Virginia innocently tells him the name of her confessor.

Comment

The consequences of Galileo's dangerous victory are becoming clear. Not only has he formally been charged with heresy, but it is clear that the Holy Office is deliberately setting traps for him. Thus Barberini puts Galileo off his guard in the hope that he will make statements, secretly recorded by the secretaries, that may be used against him. And the Cardinal Inquisitor wants to use Virginia's confessor, either to influence her against her father or, more probably, to learn from her confessor whether her father is making demonstrably heretical statements. The Confessor is, of course, bound not to reveal anything Virginia tells him in the confessional, but the Cardinal Inquisitor seems to feel that this vow presents no serious obstacle to his plan. Galileo's problem is that the Church insists on treating his scientific inquires as matters of religious concern. Galileo is not a conscious heretic, and of course modern Catholics freely accept the Copernican system which Galileo's investigations confirmed. But to the seventeenth-century churchmen, like the old Cardinal in **Scene Five** and the Inquisitor, the alleged philosophical and religious implications of Galileo's discoveries made them dangerous and required their suppression.

SCENE SEVEN

In the garden of the Florentine Ambassador, Galileo receives a visitor. It is the little monk of **Scene Five**. A student of physics, he is convinced of the rightness of Galileo's theories. Yet he regards the Holy Office's decree declaring these theories heretical a wise one. In fact, he plans to give up his own scientific research. His decision, he says, is not based on fear of the Holy Office. Rather, he thinks of the impact Galileo's discoveries may have on people like his parents. The monk is the son of poor peasants, who he says, understand the cultivation of olive trees and not much else. They have a simple faith and a simple view of the universe. But Galileo's discoveries, if permitted to be disseminated, would challenge such simple folk's view of the universe and threaten their faith, thus possibly causing them misery in this world and damnation in the next.

Galileo recognizes that there is much truth in what the monk says, but he argues that the virtues of people like the monk's parents are virtues born of misery and denies that these are the only virtues that men can achieve. Further, he insists that truth, the kind of truth he has discovered, cannot make its way alone: somebody must push it. As he argues his point, he throws down a manuscript containing a record of some of his discoveries. The monk picks it up and becomes completely absorbed in reading it. When he comes to a point he doesn't understand, he asks Galileo to explain.

Comment

As the ending of the scene indicates, the monk's dedication to science is too great to permit him to abandon his studies. He is not troubled by any conflict between reason and faith. But he is a relatively learned man as well as a devout one. His concern for simpler people like his parents is genuine. Galileo argues in effect that scientific inquiry can bring into existence a new world, one in which men will not be limited to humble virtues born of misery but will realize the new possibilities appropriate to a new and better world. Galileo's view is optimistic and expansive, while the monk's is conservative. We know that Brecht is essentially in sympathy with Galileo's point of view. It is a mark of his dramatic power that he has the opposing view eloquently and movingly expressed by a sympathetic character.

SCENE EIGHT

The setting is Galileo's house in Florence. For eight years, since the decree of the Holy Office, Galileo has kept silent. Now he, Andrea, Federzoni, and the little monk are engaged in a harmless experiment. In another part of the room, Mrs. Sarti and Virginia prepare the bridal linen, looking forward to Virginia's wedding to Ludovico. In answer to Mrs. Sarti's question, Virginia says she has had a real astronomer, not one like her father, cast her horoscope.

The philosopher of **Scene Four**, now Rector of the University, arrives to bring Galileo a book dealing with sunspots. From all over Europe, requests arrive that Galileo give his explanation for the mysterious sunspots, but Galileo refuses to speak for fear of being burned as a heretic.

After the Rector's departure Ludovico enters, having unexpectedly returned from Rome. At first Galileo doesn't recognize him; there seems to be something wrong with Galileo's eyes. Virginia, excited at her fiance's sudden appearance, leaves the room, saying she has something to show him. Ludovico has brought news from Rome. Clavius thinks that the sunspots are related to the revolutions of the earth; Galileo says nothing. Of more immediate importance, the Pope is dying, and it is generally supposed that his successor will be Barberini. Galileo is delighted. Barberini, after all, is himself a mathematician; surely he will be sympathetic to the spirit of scientific inquiry.

Galileo announces that he will now resume the study of astronomy. Moreover, he may consider writing his findings in the vernacular.

The son of a great family, Ludovico makes it clear that he is unwilling to marry the daughter of a man who may be a heretic. Moreover, he sees in Galileo's discoveries a threat to the social structure on which his family's high position is based. Seeing that Galileo will not be moved, he leaves.

When Virginia returns, Galileo and the others have already started to work. In fact. Galileo has been secretly working on the problem of the sunspots for some time, as his friends suspected when they noticed he was having trouble with his eyes. They pay no attention to Virginia. When she sees that Ludovico has gone, she realizes what has happened and falls to the floor in a faint.

Comment

There is dramatic **irony** in Galileo's confidence in Barberini's attitudes. We know, as Galileo does not, that Barberini cooperated in efforts to try to trap Galileo eight years before. The scene presents Virginia as a pathetic victim of forces she does not understand. She is not even present when Ludovico decides he cannot marry her, and her visit to the "astronomer" (what we would call an astrologer) indicates how little she understands the scientific inquiries to which she has been sacrificed.

SCENE NINE

A street scene. A street singer and his wife sing a **ballad** about Galileo's investigations. The **imagery** of the **ballad** relates

Galileo's discoveries to widespread social upheaval. This is set against an April Fool's procession (it is April 1) which features a huge figure of Galileo pointing to the Bible and shaking his head as if saying "No."

Comment

This scene shows some of the effects Galileo's discoveries are having on society as a whole. Apparently the fears of the Church and nobility were not entirely unjustified. We should not, however, assume that the relationship Brecht indicates between Galileo's discoveries and incipient social revolution is necessarily an accurate reflection of historical fact. Brecht wants us to believe, for his own dramatic and philosophical purposes, that a victory for Galileo in his struggle with authority would also have been a victory for social progress.

SCENE TEN

The setting is the place of the Medicis in Florence. Galileo's resumption of his studies in astronomy has once again led him into difficulties with the Holy Office, and he is relying on Prince Cosimo de Medici for protection. Accompanied by his daughter, he is waiting for an audience with the Prince when he is greeted by Matti, the iron founder of **Scene Two**. Matti expresses delight at seeing Galileo and hails him as a champion of human freedom. Galileo protests that his only concern is with the mechanics of the firmament. In fact, he is embarrassed and frightened to be praised in a way that makes him sound like a threat to the authority of the Church. The Lord Chamberlain enters to tell Galileo that the Prince cannot see him. Cosimo de Medici is willing to let Galileo be turned over to the Inquisition in Rome.

Comment

The Prince's decision means that Galileo has lost his only powerful protector and must now stand alone in an unequal battle with the Church. Moreover, Galileo sees he must fear his friends as well as his enemies. The kind of praise offered by the well-meaning Matti can, at this point, be as dangerous as deliberate malice.

SCENE ELEVEN

In a chamber in the Vatican, Barberini, now Pope Urban VIII, has granted an audience to the Cardinal Inquisitor. As he dons the papal robes, Barberini declares his unwillingness to have Galileo persecuted. As a learned and sophisticated man, he does not want to place the Church in the position of suppressing scientific inquiry. But the Cardinal Inquisitor argues that Galileo's discoveries lead to doubt, and the Church and society cannot stand on doubt. The Pope accepts the Inquisitor's argument but will still not permit. Galileo to be tortured. He will, however, in an attempt to frighten Galileo into a recantation permit that he be shown the instruments of torture.

Comment

This scene is yet another illustration of Brecht's mastery of the art of theater. Throughout the argument with the Inquisitor, Barberini is gradually putting on the robes of his office as Pope Urban VIII. He first speaks as a man, himself a student of the sciences and an admirer of the genius of Galileo. But as he dons his robes he becomes more and more a kind of institution, moved by an abstract sense of the interests of the Church to permit the persecution of a man he admires and a cause he respects. He becomes, in a sense, a victim of his own power, the power symbolized by the papal robes.

SCENE TWELVE

In the garden of the Florentine Ambassador at Rome, Andrea Sarti, Federzoni, the little monk, and Virginia are waiting to learn if Galileo will recant. Andrea is sure he won't; Virginia prays that he will. A man enters and informs them that Galileo is expected to announce his recantation at five o'clock; the ringing of a bell will signify the announcement. They wait breathlessly and hopefully. When five o'clock comes and no bell sounds, they rejoice. But while they are still rejoicing, the sound of a bell is heard. Galileo has recanted. Now it is Virginia who rejoices; the others are discouraged and embittered. When Galileo returns, Andrea berates him for his cowardice. "Unhappy is the land that has no heroes." he says. But Galileo replies, "Unhappy is the land that needs a hero."

Comment

Virginia's prayer is motivated by her feelings as a daughter and partly, perhaps, by her hope that her father's recantation will mean the end of her suffering. The issues of principle that concern the others mean nothing to her. In the exchange between Andrea and Galileo we observe a typically Brechtian **irony**. We admire the hero, but our need for heroes is evidence that we live in an imperfect world.

SCENE THIRTEEN

From 1633, the year of his recantation, until his death in 1642, Galileo remains a prisoner of the Inquisition. **Scene Thirteen** is set in a country house near Florence. Galileo is experimenting with a bent wooden rail and a small ball of wood.

Now almost blind, he is watched over by Virginia and an officer of the Inquisition. He is not permitted to write anything himself, but must dictate anything he wishes to record to his daughter. He is in fact permitted to continue work on his "Discorsi," the account of his discoveries, but only on condition that he will hand over each page as it is finished to the officers of the Inquisition.

Virginia, now an unmarried woman of forty, brings Galileo a goose that some unidentified person has sent him. He also has a visitor. Andrea Sarti, passing through Florence, calls to see Galileo at the request of Fabricus, an astronomer. Andrea is cool toward Galileo. Still embittered, he tells Galileo that there have been no important scientific advances in Italy since the latter submitted to the Church. Galileo expresses the hope that things may be better in the Protestant countries, but Andrea tells him that even there things are virtually at a standstill.

But Galileo has a surprise for Andrea. He has completed his "Discorsi" and has managed to conceal a copy from the eyes of the Inquisition. He gives the manuscript to Andrea and asks him to smuggle it out of the country.

Andrea now feels that he has been unjust to his old master. He now understands, he says, that Galileo had to recant in order to finish his work. But Galileo refuses to accept this excuse for his actions. The work did not need him; science does not depend on any one man. He recanted simply out of fear of being tortured. He regards himself as a traitor. If he had taken a stand, he says, an age of reason might have been inaugurated then and there. But he was too much of a coward, and so the truth must still be concealed and smuggled. Before departing, Andrea tells Galileo he is too hard on himself. After Andrea leaves, Galileo turns to eating the goose Virginia has prepared for him.

Comment

Here, as in **Scene Seven**, Brecht shows us a real moral complexity rather than preaching for a simplistic moral judgment. True, Galileo acted unheroically, but by preserving his life he succeeded in making his great contribution to human knowledge. At the same time, he did fail to meet the moral challenge with which he was faced. In earlier plays by Brecht, the idea was expressed that mere survival is the ultimate good. The statement here is far more complex, and the ultimate burden of judgment is placed on the audience.

SCENE FOURTEEN

Andrea is about to cross the border, carrying the "Discorsi." Some boys are playing outside an old woman's house, shouting that she is a witch and should be burned. Andrea lifts one of the boys up and lets him look into the woman's window to examine the evidence. The boy sees that the woman looks harmless enough, but he is still convinced that she is a witch. Telling the boy to think over what he has seen with his own eyes, Andrea departs.

Comment

Superstition dies hard. The boy prefers his old belief to the evidence of his senses. The age of reason, of which Galileo dreamed, is still to come.

GALILEO (LEBEN DES GALILEI)

CHARACTER ANALYSES

Galileo

Galileo is a man of huge appetites, appetites that extend to learning as well as to material things. Yet it must not be overlooked that Galileo loves material comforts. When we last see him he is eating, and many of his energies in the play are expended in efforts to make his life more comfortable. There is no question of his dedication to science; it even makes him a less than ideal father to his daughter. He shows no concern when Ludovico leaves in **Scene Eight**. He is at no time a conscious rebel; he wants only to be allowed to conduct his investigations without interference. Had he been more of a philosophical rebel, he might have proven more heroic when tested. But his scientific studies are a kind of indulgence, like drinking good wine or eating good food. He is not a man of principle, but a kind of intellectual hedonist. Therefore, he is unable to resist the threat - and it was only a threat - of torture. His greatness is intellectual rather than moral, as he himself understands.

Andrea Sarti

A dedicated and apt pupil of Galileo, Andrea embodies the kind of idealism his master lacks. It is this idealism that makes him despise Galileo for compromising, but it is the same idealism that leads him later to interpret Galileo's conduct more generously than Galileo himself is willing to.

Virginia

Virginia is a pathetic victim. Never understanding the issues at stake, she is transformed in the course of the play from a pretty and charming young girl to an embittered spinster acting as her father's jailer.

Ludovico Marsili

Ludovico is a mediocre and conventional young man. Coming from a noble family, he places his position before all other considerations, including his love for Virginia.

Federzoni

Galileo's assistant is an able man, although no classical scholar. He may be seen as a forerunner of the "new man" of the scientific age. Without the external trappings of aristocratic culture, he depends on his merits. Galileo certainly sees in Federzoni the hope of the future; hence his intention to write in the vernacular, in a language men like Federzoni can understand.

The Little Monk

A man torn between the demands of faith and those of science. Patently sincere, he presents Galileo with telling arguments against free scientific research, but is himself enlisted in the cause of this freedom.

Sagredo

Sagredo shares his friend Galileo's interest in science but is a more cautious and conservative man. He is genuinely disturbed by what he sees as the religious implications of Galileo's discoveries, and he is enough of a realist to predict the difficulties Galileo will encounter.

Cardinal Barberini (Pope Urban VIII)

An almost tragic figure, Barberini might have more reason than Galileo to condemn himself for failing to inaugurate an age of reason. Barberini is a learned and sophisticated man, but he is also a wily ecclesiastical politician and a conservative. In giving in to the Inquisitor, he sets in motion the chain of events leading to Galileo's recantation and the temporary defeat of the cause of free scientific inquiry. And, as he half suspects himself, his decision to support the suppression of inquiry is not even truly in the long-range interests of the Church itself.

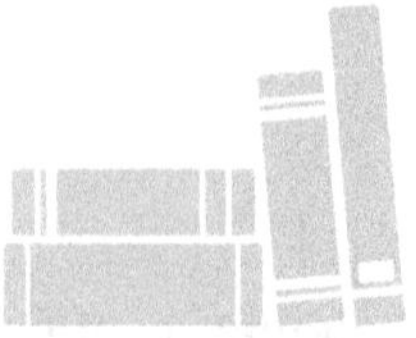

THE GOOD WOMAN OF SETZUAN (DER GUTE MENSCH VON SEZUAN)

INTRODUCTION

Both Mother Courage and Galileo, are, in a sense, divided characters. Each is torn between the demands of practical self-interest and those of nobler ideals. In *The Good Woman of Setzuan* Brecht carries the notion of the divided character one step further, presenting as his protagonist a woman who almost literally divides herself into two people, the warmhearted, generous Shen Te and her hardheaded, practical cousin Shui Ta. Brecht further implies that this sort of division is inevitable in the world in which we live, a world that will not let its Shen Te's survive unless they have the protection of Shui Ta. As a Communist, Brecht wants us to believe that in the better world to come goodness will be able to survive without the protection of cruelty. But we may choose to find more tragic implications in the picture Brecht paints for us.

CHARACTERS

Shen Te: A prostitute, later a shopkeeper, who also appears disguised as her imaginary cousin, Shui Ta.

Yang Sun: An unemployed pilot, later a factory manager; also Shen Te's lover.

Mrs. Yang: Yang Sun's mother.

Wong: A water seller.

Mrs. Shin: Former owner of Shen Te's shop.

Mrs. Mi Tzu: Shen Te's landlady.

Mr. Shu Fu: A barber, in love with Shen Te.

Three Gods: Who are looking for a good person.

A Family Of Eight: Who take advantage of Shen Te's generosity.

An Unemployed Man

A Carpenter

A Whore

A Policeman

An Old Man

An Old Woman

Gentlemen, Voices, Children, Etc.

PROLOGUE

At the gates of the city of Setzuan, Wong the water seller awaits the arrival of three gods who are supposed to be headed that way. Soon they arrive and they turn out to have some very human complaints - among them, that their feet hurt. They have been walking from city to city, looking - so far without success - for one good person. Not only have they been unable to find the good person they seek as evidence that goodness still exists in the world, but they have been unable to get any proper rest because on one has been willing to take them in at night and give them a warm and comfortable bed.

Although Wong himself is not a good person, as the gods realize when they discover a false bottom in his water cup, he promises to find the gods a place to stay in Setzuan. This proves, however, to be more difficult than he expected. Turned down by all the respectable people of Setzuan, a discouraged Wong decides he will ask the prostitute, Shen Te, to take the gods in for the night. This is an inconvenience for Shen Te, since it means she must give up an appointment with a client, but she agrees. Wong hopes only that the gods won't realize what sort of woman they're staying with.

Next morning the gods prepare to take their leave, satisfied that in Shen Te they've found the good person they're looking for. She denies she's good, pointing out she sells herself for money, but the gods reject her arguments. In payment for her hospitality, and to help her meet the expenses of a more virtuous way of life, they give her money and depart.

Comment

Two **themes** important to the play are introduced in this prologue. The first is the scarcity of goodness in the world. The second is the ineffectuality and irrelevance of the gods, whom Brecht treats as objects of ridicule. Their refusal to accept Shen Te's low evaluation of herself seems based less on divine charity than on expediency. If they can claim that Shen Te is the good person they've been seeking, they have an excuse for giving up their tiresome wanderings and resuming the comfortable life proper to gods.

THE GOOD WOMAN OF SETZUAN (DER GUTE MENSCH VON SEZUAN)

SCENE SYNOPSES

SCENE ONE

With the money from the three gods, Shen Te has purchased a tobacco shop from a Mrs. Shin, who continues to hang about the shop and expects Shen Te to give her handouts of rice and cash. The good-natured Shen Te finds it impossible to refuse Mrs. Shin's demands.

Mrs. Shin is not the only one to take advantage of Shen Te's generosity. A husband and wife and their nephew soon arrive, asking Shen Te to put them up. They remind her that they took her in when she needed help. (Actually, they exploited and overworked her in the tobacco shop they used to own.) And soon after this an unemployed man wanders in, asking for a handout of cigarettes. At this point Mrs. Shen and the others warn Shen Te that she must not allow herself to be taken advantage of. If she finds it difficult to refuse those who ask for charity, the husband advises, she should pretend the shop belongs to a relative who refuses to let her give anything away.

A carpenter arrives to demand payment for the shelves he installed. Shen Te, who was assured that Mrs. Shin had already paid for the shelves, has no money for the carpenter. Following the husband's advice, she instructs the carpenter to leave his bill for her "cousin," who takes care of such matters.

The parade of new arrivals is not over yet. The wife's brother and pregnant sister-in-law turn up, also expecting to be taken in by Shen Te. Mrs. Mi Tzu, the landlady, arrives to announce she requires references from Shen Te. Still maintaining the deception proposed by the husband, Shen Te refers Mrs. Mi Tzu to her prosperous cousin, Shui Ta, who lives in Shung. This satisfies Mrs. Mi Tzu for the time being.

Eventually the husband, wife, nephew, brother, and sister-in-law are joined by the rest of their family, bringing the total to eight. They help themselves to Shen Te's cigarettes and wine. A family quarrel develops, in the course of which considerable damage is done to Shen Te's shop.

Comment

In this scene we see what may be a partial explanation of the gods' difficulty in finding a good person. The truly good person, like Shen Te, is at the mercy of others who take advantage of his goodness. This being so, who can afford to be good? The good person could survive only in a perfect world.

SCENE ONE (A)

The three gods visit Wong's den, located in a sewer pipe. They tell him of the goodness they have found in Shen Te and order him to find her, see how she is doing, and report back to them.

SCENE TWO

Back at the shop, the family of eight is still living on Shen Te's charity. But they are greedy enough to want still more and send one of their number out to steal for them. What they don't know is that Shen Te has taken to heart the husband's advice that she pretend the shop really belongs to a relative. Shen Te arrives disguised as a man-Shui Ta, cousin of Shen Te.

Shui Ta argues with the carpenter over his bill for the shelves and, by driving a harder bargain than the meek Shen Te could have done, forces the carpenter to accept far less than his original demands. Shui Ta also orders the family of eight out of the shop. When they ignore his order, Shen Te summons a policeman. Since they are waiting to receive stolen goods, the family realize they had better leave, but before they can do so, the boy they sent out returns with what he has stolen. Sizing up the situation, the policeman takes the whole family away.

Mrs. Mi Tzu arrives, disturbed by all the commotion. She runs a respectable house, she says, and if Shen Te's activities are going to bring in the police, respectability demands payment of six months' rent in advance. Not even Shui Ta's craftiness can help in this situation, since the money is simply not available. But the policeman, returning and becoming aware of the problem, has a suggestion: let Shen Te advertise for a wealthy husband.

Comment

It is ironic that the imaginary relative, originally the idea of the husband, should be turned so quickly against the husband and his family. We can take unmixed pleasure in seeing this greedy family getting what it deserves, for we recognize that the husband's suggestion to Shen Te was not motivated by concern for her, but by fear that others might receive the fruits of generosity he wanted to enjoy.

Things are rather more complicated with regard to the Carpenter, however. If his original demands are excessive, Shui Ta's final settlement is unreasonably meager. Shui Ta does not hesitate to take advantage of the Carpenter when the opportunity presents itself. Like other Brechtian characters Shen Te/Shui Ta is undergoing a painful process of education. She is learning how many tricks one must master if one is to survive in this world.

SCENE THREE

In the park at evening, Shen Te encounters the unemployed pilot, Yang Sun. Despair at his inability to find work has brought Yang Sun to the point of committing suicide, but Shen Te argues him out of this. When Wong comes along, complaining that, because it is raining, no one will buy his water, Shen Te buys a cup and gives it to Yang Sun. She stays with the young pilot, and it is clear that she has fallen in love with him.

Comment

It is entirely consistent with what we have seen of Shen Te's character that she fall in love with a young man who is in despair, and that she first express her love by giving him water. It is, in fact, unlikely that Shen Te could love a man capable of standing on his own two feet. It is also typical of Shen Te's impracticality that she buys a cup of water when it is raining.

SCENE THREE (A)

Again the gods come to Wong's den in the sewer pipe to inquire about the fortunes of Shen Te. Wong tells them that Shen Te seems to be doing rather well, on the whole, and has fallen in love. The gods are eager to be kept informed of Shen Te's progress and are also full of complaints about the wickedness of people. Wong suggests that the gods may be judging people by standards that are too harsh.

Comment

In the role of tolerant moralist he here assumes, Wong may well be acting as Brecht's spokesman, arguing that in a world as imperfect as ours, moral perfection is an irrelevant and frustrating ideal. At any rate, within the framework of the play, Wong seems more in touch with reality than do the gods, who show no interest in recognizing thins as they are.

SCENE FOUR

The setting is the square in front of Shen Te's tobacco shop. Mrs. Shin and some of the others gossip about Shen Te's morals. She has stayed out all night; is she reverting to her old ways? While they talk, Shu Fu, the barber, whose shop is next to Shen Te's, ejects Wong from his shop, injuring the water seller's hand in the process.

Shen Te arrives in the square. Seeing her, Shu Fu becomes convinced that he is falling in love with her. Shen Te's neighbors, an old couple, offer to lend her the two hundred dollars she needs for the rent. She gratefully accepts their offer. Meanwhile, Wong finds that none of the witnesses of what has happened to him will testify on his behalf if he brings a complaint against Shu Fu. Sympathizing with Wong, Shen Te, who didn't see what happened, agrees to perjure herself for him.

Yang Sun's mother arrives to tell Shen Te the good news: Yang Sun has a chance at a job. The only trouble is that he needs five hundred dollars or the job won't be his. Shen Te gives Mrs. Yang the two hundred she has received from the old couple. She decides she will have to summon Shui Ta once again to raise the additional three hundred.

Comment

When Shen Te gives Mrs. Yang the money she has just received from the old couple, we have a right to think she is not only kind but foolishly imprudent. Her impulses are good but uncontrolled. In seeking to aid Yang Sun she runs the risk of hurting the old couple who have generously come to her assistance.

Notice also that Shen Te's goodness is a matter of benevolence rather than adherence to any sort of strict moral code. For the sake of doing Wong a favor, she is willing to commit perjury. And, however laudable her motives, in testifying to something she hasn't seen. Shen Te will hardly be acting fairly towards Shu Fu. In a complex world, perhaps the simple good will of Shen Te is not the best answer, after all.

SCENE FOUR (A)

Shen Te, carrying the mask of Shui Ta, sings a song in which she laments that the good are unable to defend themselves in this world and that it is impossible to help one person without hurting a dozen others at the same time.

Comment

The song suggests that Shen Te, like many of Brecht's other characters, is undergoing a process of education. She is becoming faintly aware of the lessons implied in **Scene Four**.

SCENE FIVE

In the shop Shui Ta sits reading a newspaper while Mrs. Shin cleans the shop. Mrs. Shin mentions to Shui Ta that the prosperous barber Shu Fu is interested in Shen Te.

Yang Sun arrives and explains to Shui Ta that he needs five hundred dollars to give to the director of an airfield in Peking in exchange for a job. Part of the deal is that the director will fire another man to make way for Yang Sun. Yang Sun is not at all interested in staying in Setzuan and selling cigars in Shen Te's shop. To raise the money for Yang Sun, Shui Ta tries to sell the shop to Mrs. Mi Tzu for five hundred dollars. She offers three hundred. Yang Sun can't understand why Shui Ta doesn't accept, since three hundred, together with the two hundred Shen Te already gave his mother, will give him the five hundred he needs, but Shui Ta is thinking of the two hundred that must be paid back to the old couple. Yang Sun makes it clear that he has no intention of marrying Shen Te, but he instructs Shui Ta to accept the three hundred, deceive Shen Te into thinking he intends to marry her, and tell her to bring the money to him. Taking a few of Shen Te's cigars, Yang Sun leaves.

Shu Fu enters and tells Shui Ta of his interest in Shen Te. He says he knows how much of a drain Shen Te's charities have been on her finances and offers to support her charitable activities. Seeing in Shu Fu a useful source of money, Shui Ta encourages him. But at this moment Wong and a policeman arrive, looking for Shen Te to testify against Shu Fu. Wong is dismayed, and Shu Fu is delighted, when Shui Ta says Shen Te will not give testimony. The policeman takes Wong away, and Shui Ta goes into the back room, telling Shu Fu he will find Shen Te.

Yang Sun returns and a gloating Shu Fu says he and Shen Te will soon announce their engagement. But when Shen Te comes out of the back room, she goes off with Yang Sun.

Comment

It is a peculiar feature of Shen Te's character that she seems to learn nothing from her experience as Shui Ta. The two halves of her personality remain completely divided. Thus, even though Shui Ta encourages Shu Fu, because this is the practical thing to do, Shen Te impractically leaves with the faithless and unworthy Yang Sun.

SCENE FIVE (A)

Going to her wedding to Yang Sun, Shen Te learns that the old man from whom she borrowed two hundred dollars is ill, and she has promised his wife she'll return the money at once.

Comment

By this time we may begin to recognize in Shen Te's inability to refuse a request some resemblance to Galy Gay, the **protagonist** of *A Man's a Man.*

SCENE SIX

The guests have gathered for Shen Te's wedding to Yang Sun, but the prospective bride and groom quarrel when Shen Te mentions her desire to give two hundred dollars to the old couple. Besides, he insists the wedding can't begin until Shui Ta arrives. Eventually the priest and guests become impatient and leave, seeing that no wedding will take place this day.

Comment

This scene reinforces our impression of Yang Sun's worthlessness and Shen Te's masochism. It also indicates the degree to which Shui Ta is becoming important in the life of Shen Te.

SCENE SIX (A)

The gods pay another visit to Wong. Although he tells them of Shen Te's difficulties, they refuse to intervene. It is not their business, they say, to become involved in the affairs of humans.

Comment

The gods refusal to help Shen Te in spite of her goodness confirms their complete indifference to human problems.

SCENE SEVEN

Behind Shen Te's shop, Shu Fu, still as interested in her as ever, brings Shen Te a blank check and tells her to fill in whatever amount she needs for her good works. When Shu Fu leaves, Wong appears with a child. The child is the carpenter's; the carpenter has taken to drink and abandoned his family. Shen Te agrees to help Wong and to take care of the carpenter's children. She is pregnant herself now, and the sight of this miserable child makes her resolve always to be good to her son and to be a tigress to others.

Comment

Shen Te's pregnancy is teaching her a lesson she never learned from Shui Ta's experiences: in a cruel and selfish world one must be cruel and selfish to protect oneself and those one loves.

Shen Te's yard fills up. Some members of the family of eight bring stolen tobacco and demand that Shen Te hide it for them.

The carpenter arrives with two more of his children. Mrs. Shin and others arrive. But Shen Te once again assumes the disguise of Shui Ta. Shui Ta refuses to take care of the carpenter's children, but offers the carpenter a job. Since he plans to claim the stolen tobacco for himself and run his factory, Shui Ta needs workers. Picking up the blank check left by Shu Fu, Shui Ta makes if out for ten thousand dollars to pay off Mrs. Mi Tzu. When the old couple arrive, looking for Shen Te, they are told she isn't there. Mrs. Shin, meanwhile, has begun to notice a few things and suspects Shui Ta may be Shen Te in disguise.

Comment

In his efforts on Shen Te's behalf Shui Ta is becoming increasingly aggressive. But this is necessary because Shen Te's difficulties are becoming more acute, and provision must be made for the child she expects.

SCENE SEVEN (A)

When the gods visit him, Wong asks them to relax their rules, substituting more attainable ideals for the impossible ones they insist on. The gods refuse.

SCENE EIGHT

The setting is Shui Ta's factory, located in huts Shu Fu had originally Provided for Shen Te's charitable activities. Mrs. Yang speaks enthusiastically of what Shui Ta has done for her son, Yang Sun, over the past three months. He has transformed Yang Sun into a model citizen.

Three months before Shui Ta brought a breach of promise suit against Yang Sun and accused him of having come by two hundred dollars improperly. He then offered to let Sun make up for what he had done by going to work in the tobacco factory. Now Sun is a foreman who drives his men unmercifully - a model citizen.

Comment

Shui Ta's harshness has achieved what Shen Te's kindness could never have done: made a respectable man out of Yang Sun. Note, however, that Yang Sun's moral character has not improved at all; he is still as selfish and ruthless as ever.

SCENE NINE

Shen Te's shop has been turned into an office with comfortable chairs and fine carpets. Shui Ta is now being looked after by Mrs. Shin, who knows that Shui Ta is really Shen Te, now in the seventh month of her pregnancy. It is Shen Te's hope that her child will never learn of Shui Ta.

Comment

It is apparently Shen Te's hope that her son will be victimized by the same illusions that have caused her so much difficulty. He must never know of Shui Ta; but Shui Ta, as Shen Te should know, is a part of reality.

Yang Sun comes to the office and tells Shui Ta that the factory's present facilities are inadequate. They will have to expand into buildings owned by Mrs. Mi Tzu. Sun offers to become Mrs. Mi Tzu's lover to make her agree to let them use the building. At first Shui Ta, reacting with Shen Te's feelings, refuses to consider this. But then he agrees.

Wong arrives, looking for Shen Te. He reveals that when he last saw her she told him she was pregnant. Now he's afraid of what might have happened to her. Seeing his opportunity, Yang Sun threatens to bring the police to search for Shen Te unless Shui Ta makes him top man. When Sun returns with the police, they discover some of Shen Te's clothes, and Shui Ta is charged with the murder of Shen Te.

SCENE NINE (A)

When the gods visit Wong again, their appearance shows clearly that they have suffered harsh treatment in their wanderings through the world. And they are discouraged. Shen Te is the only really good person they've found, and now no one seems to know where she is.

SCENE TEN

The settings in court. Shui Ta, on trial for murder, almost faints when he sees the three gods appear in judges robes. The trial commences. Shui Ta's character is praised by the policeman, Shu Fu, and Mrs. Mi Tzu, but he is attacked by many others, including Wong, the old couple, the carpenter, and the thieving family.

Comment

The harsh, businesslike Shui Ta is praised by the symbols of wealth and authority in society and attacked by society's victims and outcasts.

Scene Ten (Continued)

Speaking in his own behalf, Shui Ta says that he always acted in Shen Te's interests and was her only true friend. He then asks that the courtroom be cleared. When his request has been carried out, he removes his disguise and reveals himself to the gods as Shen Te. When Shen Te points out that her good actions have had bad consequences, they merely tell her to go on being good. When she protests that she cannot survive without the wicked Shui Ta, they say it may be permissible to use Shui Ta occasionally - say, once a month. Ascending into heaven on a pink cloud, they leave a troubled Shen Te alone.

Comment

The decision of the gods solves nothing; Shen Te is left with the problem of how a good person is to survive in a bad world. If the world is to be fit for its good people, it must be remade - by men, not by gods.

EPILOGUE

Abandoned by the gods, Shen Te turns to the audience, states the problem directly to them, and asks what is to be done.

Comment

From Brecht's point of view, Shen Te's question is merely rhetorical. The answer, which the audience is expected to recognize, is that a Communist revolution is necessary to bring into existence a world in which it will be possible for men to be good. But for those of us who are skeptical about the adequacy of the Marxist formula, or any formula, for Utopia, Shen Te's question is a real one. Will it ever be possible for men to be truly good and not be destroyed by their goodness?

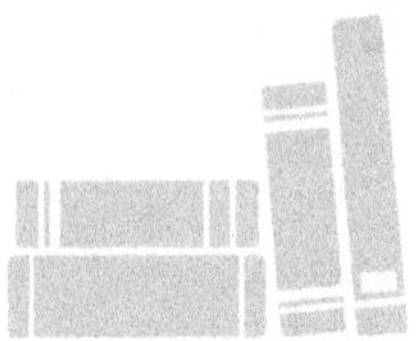

THE GOOD WOMAN OF SETZUAN (DER GUTE MENSCH VON SEZUAN)

CHARACTER ANALYSES

Shen Te

Shen Te is a woman of good and generous impulses, but she is also unrealistic in her attitudes. She even hopes that her child will never know of the harsh realities she has had to face, even though this would seem to mean that he would be as ill-equipped to cope with the world as she. In her relation with Yang Sun, Shen Te goes beyond generosity to what approaches masochism.

Shui Ta

Shen Te's imaginary cousin and protector. Shui Ta must do the cruel things that Shen Te is unable to do in her own person; otherwise Shen Te's generosity would lead to her total ruin. This division of personality into two halves is obviously not an adequate solution to the problem of evil, as Shen Te herself finally realizes.

Wong

Although he is not a "good person" by the standards of the gods, Wong is an instinctive moralist of natural good sense. When he suggests to the gods that their standards are too rigid, he is implicitly preaching a morality adjusted to the needs of an imperfect world.

Yang Sun

Shen Te's lover is a selfish and unscrupulous young man. Shen Te loves him for his weakness, but he proves himself capable of surviving in the harsh world of Shui Ta. It is an indictment of this world that it treats a Yang Sun better than it treats a Shen Te.

The Three Gods

The gods are absurd in their ineptitude and in their obstinate refusal to recognize the realities of the world in which men must live. In the framework of Brecht's thought, they symbolize the folly of man's looking beyond himself for assistance in dealing with his problems.

THE CAUCASIAN CHALK CIRCLE (DER KAUKASISCHE KREIDEKREIS)

INTRODUCTION

The Caucasian Chalk Circle is the last of Brecht's masterpieces. Although he continued to write after completing this work in 1945, most critics agree that his later works, while not without interest, do not indicate any significant further developments in his art.

In structure, *The Caucasian Chalk Circle* employs the traditional device of the play within a play. The rather crudely **didactic** framework involves a dispute over land rights. The central action, the play within a play, is offered to the disputing parties as a model, a guide to what their decision means. The climactic scene, the test of the circle, is a reworking of a traditional story, one version of which is familiar to the Judaic-Christian audience as an example of the wisdom of Solomon. It is typical of Brecht that he twists the moral of this familiar tale to suit his own purposes.

For many of us, the greatness of *The Caucasian Chalk Circle* lies less in its narrative structure and philosophical implications than in the unforgettable vitality of the characters. Grusha and Azdak belong with Mother Courage and Galileo in Brecht's gallery of memorable creations.

CHARACTERS OF THE PROLOGUE

The Story Teller: Who knows a story that will help settle the argument over land rights.

Delegate: Of the State Reconstruction Commission, from the Capital.

Peasants, Agriculturists, Tractorists, Etc.: Disputants in the argument.

CHARACTERS OF THE PLAY

Georgi Abashwili: The governor.

Natella: His wife.

Michael: Their son.

Shalva: An attendant.

Arsen: Kazbeki A fat prince.

Messenger: From the Capital.

Doctors: Niko Makadze, Mika Loladze

Simon Shashava: A Soldier.

Grusha Vashnadze: A kitchen maid.

Old Peasant: Who has milk.

Corporal and Private: Who harass Grusha.

Peasant and Wife: Who fears the ironshirts.

Lavrenti Washmadze: Grusha's brother.

Aniko: His wife.

Peasant: Woman Who becomes Grusha's mother-in-law.

Jussup: Her son, who becomes Grusha's husband.

Monk: Who performs weddings and funerals.

Azdak: Village recorder.

Disputants in cases tried by Azdak: Doctor, Innkeeper, Invalid, Stable Boy, Limping Man, Poor Old Peasant Woman, Blackmailer, Irakli (a bandit), Ludovica, Three Wealthy Farmers

Lawyers: Illo Shuboladze, Sandro Oboladze.

Old Married Couple: Who want a divorce.

Soldiers, Servants, Etc.

PROLOGUE

The setting is a Caucasian village ruined by the effects of World War II. A delegate from the Capital is trying to settle a dispute between two groups, each of which wants to be allowed to settle in the village. One of the groups wants to use the land for dairy farming, the other for viniculture. After some discussion, it is agreed the land should go to the second group. The Story Teller is then invited to perform. He says he will put on a play that may have some bearing on the day's deliberations.

Comment

As was indicated in the Introduction, the device of the play written within a play is a traditional one. It also is consistent with Brecht's theory of "alienation." The story of Grusha is presented to us at one remove; we are reminded it is made up; and we are invited, rather than losing ourselves in it, to remain alert to its meaning.

In style, the prologue resembles the "socialist **realism**" which constituted aesthetic orthodoxy in the regime of Stalin and is still of importance in countries behind the Iron Curtain. Brecht has sometimes been attacked by Communist critics on grounds that his "**epic** theatre" is inconsistent with socialist realism.

THE CAUCASIAN CHALK CIRCLE (DER KAUKASISCHE KREIDEKREIS)

TEXTUAL ANALYSIS

ACT ONE

The story is set many years ago in a Caucasian city and begins one Easter Sunday. With much bustle and ado, the Governor, Georgi Abashwili, and his wife, Natella, prepare to go to church, bringing with them their infant son, Michael. On the way, they receive an unctuous greeting from the fat Prince Kazbeki. What they don't know is that the Prince is involved in a revolution which that very day will bring about the overthrow and death of the Governor.

But not everyone in the city is concerned with pomp and politics. Simon Shashava, a young soldier, chats merrily with Grusha, a kitchen maid. Their pleasant conversation is interrupted, however, by the outbreak of the revolution. The Governor has been arrested, his wife deserted by many of her retainers. Simon must follow her into exile as her guard. He asks Grusha to wait for him and to marry him on his return. Grusha promises she will do as he asks.

The cruelty and selfishness of the Governor's wife are revealed as, in looking out for her own safety, she completely forgets about her son, Michael, who in the excitement is handed to Grusha. Grusha realizes that it would be dangerous for her to be found with the Governor's son, especially after she sees the Governor's head carried on a lance. Not knowing what to do, she watches with the child through the night. In the morning, unable to resist the temptation to perform a good act, she takes the child away with her.

Comment

The **satire** in the presentation of the Governor, the wife, and the Prince, while done with skill, is rather broad.

They are essentially caricatures. A more natural quality is introduced as Brecht turns to the sympathetic characters, Simon and Grusha. They are little people, the victims of the intrigues of powerful and greedy men. Because of plots and counterplots that mean nothing to them, they are separated. The poignant problem of such people is that their happiness depends so much on forces outside themselves.

Note that Grusha's decision to take care of Michael is presented as yielding to a temptation. It is Brecht's unusual, but stimulating, contention that we avoid doing good only by dint of intense, if misguided, effort. Each of us would be good if we weren't careful.

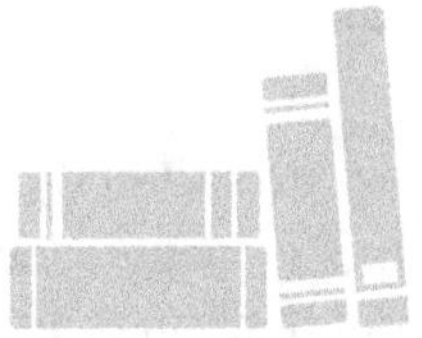

THE CAUCASIAN CHALK CIRCLE (DER KAUKASISCHE KREIDEKREIS)

TEXTUAL ANALYSIS

ACT TWO

Having left the city, Grusha walks toward the Northern Mountains, carrying the child on her back. Approaching a peasant's hut, she decides to buy some milk for the child. Seeing in Grusha's need the opportunity to make a profit, the old peasant who owns the hut charges her an excessive price for the little milk he gives her.

Grusha must keep moving, for the ironshirts - soldiers - are following her, looking for the Governor's child, whom they want to kill. Grusha thinks she had better leave the child with someone who can care for him properly. She places him on the doorstep of a peasant's hut and watches the peasant woman when she comes out and finds the child. Grusha is relieved that the woman and her husband are pleased to find a child on their doorstep and are willing to take care of it. Yet she also feels sad at giving up the child.

As she walks back towards the city, Grusha encounters two ironshirts, a corporal and a private, who are looking for the Governor's child. Alarmed, she runs back to warn the peasant and his wife of the ironshirts' approach and to beg them not to reveal where the baby came from. But when the ironshirts arrive, the frightened wife blurts out the whole story. Grusha is forced to knock out the corporal in order to escape with Michael.

Still pursued by the ironshirts, Grusha, who now considers Michael her adopted son, comes to a rotten bridge. People standing by warn her that it is impossible to cross the bridge, that if she tries she will fall into the abyss. But, rather than let Michael fall into the hands of the ironshirts, Grusha decides to try it. The bridge holds, and Grusha and Michael get safely to the other side just as the ironshirts arrive, led by the Corporal, whose bandaged head shows the effect of Grusha's blow. Since the bridge that barely supported Grusha obviously won't support them, the ironshirts must watch helplessly as Grusha happily carries Michael away.

Comment

Her growing devotion to the child leads Grusha more and more to assume the role and responsibilities of a mother, to the point where she will risk her own life before she will let anything happen to the child. Although he is cynical about many of the old-fashioned virtues, Brecht treats mother love with respect. By her devotion to the child, which contrasts sharply with the behavior of the child's real mother, Grusha is earning the right to claim it as her own.

It should be remembered that the Story Teller and the others from the Prologue remain visible throughout the play, commenting on the action as it proceeds. It is, for example, through their comments that we learn Grusha's feelings after she has left the child with the peasants. This contributes to a certain "distancing" or "alienation" of the action. We are not invited to share Grusha's feelings, but to observe them.

Grusha reveals herself in this act not only as warm-hearted, but as tough and resourceful when the occasion demands. Unlike the passive Shen Te of *The Good Woman of Setzuan*, Grusha realizes that one must at times act firmly in defense of those one loves. She is able to cope with her predicament more effectively than Shen Te could have done.

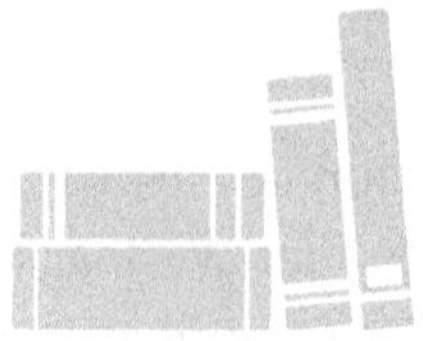

THE CAUCASIAN CHALK CIRCLE (DER KAUKASISCHE KREIDEKREIS)

TEXTUAL ANALYSIS

ACT THREE

Grusha is heading for the home of her brother in the Northern Mountains, where, the Story Teller informs us, she expects a warm welcome. But she is in part disappointed. Her brother, Lavrenti, is glad to see her, but he must think of the feelings of his wife, Aniko. They both believe the child is Grusha's, born out of wedlock, and Aniko is narrow-minded about such things. Moreover, when Grusha faints from exhaustion, Aniko fears she has brought a disease with her. But in spite of his wife's resistance, Lavrenti's brotherly feelings require that he give shelter to his sister.

Comment

A consistent function of the Story Teller and the chorus that assists him is to inform us directly of the feelings of the characters in the play. In **Act Two**, they told us of Grusha's feelings when she left the child. In this act they tell us of Grusha's expectations as she comes to her brother's house, and of Lavrenti's feelings as he decides he must help his sister.

Act Three (Continued)

After Grusha and Michael have been living with him for about six months, Lavrenti comes to Grusha with news: he has found a husband for her. This will give Grusha respectability and, at the same time, get her and the child off Lavrenti's hands. Grusha, of course, does not want to marry anybody since she is still waiting for Simon.

But Lavrenti points out that the man he has in mind is on his death bed; the marriage will be purely a matter of form. Furthermore, as part of the arrangement, Grusha and Michael will be able to live for two years on the farm owned by the dying man's mother. On these terms, Grusha agrees.

The wedding ceremony is an odd one, since it is also in part a funeral service for the dying bridegroom, Jussup, and the guests are prematurely nibbling on the funeral meats, Jussup's mother, who has been paid by Lavrenti for her part in the transaction, has hired a monk to perform the ceremony. Monks don't charge as much as priests. After the wedding ceremony has ended, some of the guests mention the news that the war has ended. At this, Jussup sits up in bed, obviously quite healthy. He has been pretending to be ill in order to avoid being called into the army.

In spite of this deception, Grusha recognizes her obligation to live up to the terms of the agreement and lives with Jussup as his wife. Although he is a crude and selfish man, she wastes no time in self-pity. One day as Grusha is washing linen in a stream,

Simon arrives. Not knowing the whole story, he simply thinks Grusha has been unfaithful to him. The Story Teller explains to us the profound feelings that Simon and Grusha are unable to express. They are suddenly surprised by the sound of shouting. The soldiers have come and taken Michael away.

Comment

It is a further sign of Grusha's strength that she accepts her condition without complaint, even though she has been deceived. It is therefore doubly bitter that, in spite of her efforts, the soldiers find her and take Michael away. Her unselfishness is made more emphatic by contrast with Jussup and his mother. She seems to recognize instinctively that people like herself must always expect to be victims of circumstances. All they can do is make the best of their situation. But, as we have seen, in what concerns the child Grusha goes beyond a stoic's acceptance of fate to an active struggle against circumstances. We do not expect her to accept the loss of Michael without a fight.

THE CAUCASIAN CHALK CIRCLE (DER KAUKASISCHE KREIDEKREIS)

TEXTUAL ANALYSIS

ACT FOUR (PART TWO, ACT ONE, IN SOME VERSIONS)

The scene shifts back to the Easter Sunday on which the revolution began. Azdak, the Village Recorder, finds a fugitive, an old man, wandering in the woods and gives him shelter. The old man offers to pay Azdak 150,000 piasters if he will shelter him and help him to escape. But when Shauwa the policemen arrives, the old man fears Azdak will turn him in. Actually, Shauwa has come to arrest Azdak for killing a rabbit. Which is worse, Azdak demands, a rabbit-catcher like himself or a man-catcher like Shauwa? The bewildered Shauwa leaves with neither Azdak nor the old man.

The old man is in fact the Grand Duke, fleeing from the insurrection, but even when he discovers this, Azdak doesn't turn him over to the police, either out of contempt for them or sympathy for the old man. Afterwards, however, Azdak feels ashamed of having helped the corrupt old official and, dragging

Shauwa behind him, arrives in the city of Nuka, demanding punishment for what he has done. But the ironshirts to whom he turns himself in are indifferent to what he has to say. Besides, since the judge has been hanged, there's no one to try Azdak. Prince Kazbeki brings his dull-witted nephew to the courtroom. Here, he says, is a young man who would make an excellent judge, but the ironshirts may decide for themselves. They decide to hold a tryout, with the Prince's nephew acting as judge and Azdak as the accused. As a result of the tryout, they make Azdak the judge.

Azdak turns out to be an unconventional judge. He readily accepts bribes from rich people, but his verdicts are unpredictable. A poor woman is accused of having accepted a leg of pork from a bandit. Azdak rules that the leg of pork must have flown into her window by a miracle, and says those who disagree are guilty of godlessness and disbelief in miracles. In another case a buxom young woman has accused a man of raping her. But when Azdak notices how she swings her bottom when she walks, he finds her guilty of assault with a deadly weapon and takes her to the stable to "examine the scene of the crime."

Comment

In an era of confusion and disorder Azdak acts as a lord of misrule. His judgments are patently absurd. Yet there is a peculiar kind of justice in them. Normally it would require some sort of miracle for a poor woman to get decent food to eat. The responsibility for this lies with the wealthy men who have brought charges against her, but there is, in ordinary jurisprudence, no way to make them pay for their mistreatment of the poor. Azdak's judgment, then, while absurd with regard to the specific charge, is just with regard to the deeper crime committed by the rich against the poor.

Act Four (Continued)

The political situation changes once again. Prince Kazbeki and his allies are turned out of office, the Grand Duke returns to power and Natella, the Governor's wife, returns, looking now for the child she had abandoned before. When she tells her story to Azdak, the judge, he promises, that the child will be found and the girl who claims him as her own will be beheaded.

Comment

The return of Natella explains how it happens that the soldiers took Michael away at the end of **Act Three**. Azdak's attempt to ingratiate himself with Natella, now that she has power once again, is as much a part of his character as his peculiar sense of justice. Although he has great vitality, Azdak is in no sense a heroic figure.

Until its closing moments, **Act Four** seems to take us far from the story of Grusha and the child. What is its function? First of all, of course, it introduces us to the character of Azdak, who, as the closing moments suggest, will play an important role in Grusha's story. Secondly, by its quality of unreality, it casts a new light on Grusha's story. It is only in the crazy world in which an Azdak can become a judge that people like Grusha have a chance of being treated justly. In the real world, Brecht implies, society is ordered for the protection of the rich and powerful minority - the Natellas - and for the suppression and persecution of the poor majority. It is only through the ascent of disorder that the poor have a chance. In the design of the play as a whole, all this is in contrast to the "true" justice - from Brecht's point of view -of Communist society, as presented in the Prologue.

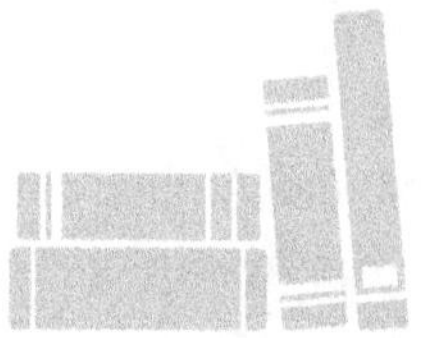

THE CAUCASIAN CHALK CIRCLE (DER KAUKASISCHE KREIDEKREIS)

TEXTUAL ANALYSIS

ACT FIVE

The day of the trial to determine into whose custody the child will be placed has arrived. Grusha has little reason to hope, although Simon offers to swear that he is the child's father. She is at first alarmed to see among those present the Corporal she encountered on her way to the Northern Mountains. But then she realizes he can't testify against her, since to do so he would have to admit he had been pursuing Natella's child with the intention of killing it.

The trial is delayed as everyone awaits the arrival of the judge who is to be appointed by the Grand Duke. Azdak is no longer a judge, for he has been denounced as an enemy of the Grand Duke and is in fact about to be hanged - much to the delight of Natella, who has disliked him from the moment she met him. But a messenger arrives to announce that Azdak has been appointed to the judgeship by the Grand Duke himself, who remembers the service Azdak rendered him in the early days of the revolution. Ttus Azdak will hear the case after all.

In his usual fashion Azdak makes clear to the rich Natella that he is willing to accept bribes and speaks harshly to Grusha, who has no money to offer. Grusha berates Azdak for his apparent corruption and heartlessness. As the trial proceeds, it becomes clear that Natella's interest in getting the child is not the result of mother love but of the fact that she wants control over the estate that Michael has inherited from his father. Azdak asks Grusha if she wouldn't like her child to be rich. She replies that to be rich is to be cruel.

Comment

In this first encounter between Grusha and Azdak, the two central characters of the play, we see the contrast between Grusha's unyielding heroism and Azdak's pragmatic timeserving. To be sure, Azdak will finally decide in Grusha's favor, but in a better world Grusha would not have to depend on a man like Azdak.

Act V (Continued)

Finally Azdak proposes that the test of the chalk circle be employed. The child is to be placed in a center of a circle. Natella and Grusha are each to take one of his arms and pull. The child will go, says Azdak, to the one who pulls him out of the circle. When the time comes, Grusha cannot pull for fear of injuring the child. Azdak rules that this feeling proves she is the child's true mother and awards Michael to Grusha.

Meanwhile, an old couple has come to court to apply for a divorce. By "mistake" Azdak divorces Grusha from Jussup instead, thus freeing her to marry Simon. The Story Teller says that after that evening Azdak disappeared, but long afterward people remembered the time when Azdak was judge as a brief golden age, almost an age of justice.

The Story Teller then points out the moral of the story. What there is should go to those who are good for it. Children should go to the motherly, and the land should go to those who will make it fruitful.

Comment

The time when Azdak was judge was only "almost" an age of justice, because it was based only on the whims of an unpredictable man who was at least half a scoundrel. Yet the comment of the Story Teller implies that this was closer to a true age of justice than any other time the people had ever known. What is suggested is that true justice is rare indeed.

THE CAUCASIAN CHALK CIRCLE (DER KAUKASISCHE KREIDEKREIS)

CHARACTER ANALYSES

Grusha

Grusha is one of Brecht's good people, differing from some others like Kattrin and Shen Te in that she is not merely passive but capable of acting and speaking boldly in her own behalf. Her central motivation is her devotion to the child. She will let her lover think her unfaithful rather than risk betraying the child to his enemies. And she will risk her own life for the sake of her child. In fact, she seldom thinks of herself at all. She does not indulge in self-pity after being deceived by Jussup, and she gives no indication of regarding herself as unusually virtuous.

Azdak

As an unorthodox judge who somehow manages consistently to arrive at wise decisions. Azdak implicitly criticizes in his actions our conventional notions of justice. If there is any consistent principle in his decisions, it seems to be that the guilt of the individual is less important than the guilt of society. If a poor woman just accepts a stolen piece of meat, the crime is not against society but against her. If his procedures and decisions seem unorthodox, it is because in his view the issues to be decided are not the superficial ones understood by lawyers, but deeper ones touching on the basic circumstances of man's condition. For all his instinctive wisdom, however, Azdak is not a heroic figure. Unlike Grusha, Azdak never loses sight of his own interests. Hence, his willingness to accept bribes and to adapt himself to whatever changes may occur in the political structure of the state. It may be that Azdak's apparent cynicism in so many matters has something to do with his discovery, when he tried to give himself up for helping the Grand Duke, of the indifference with which such matters are regarded. In a better world Grusha would not have had to depend on Azdak - and perhaps Azdak would not have had to be Azdak.

Natella Abashwili

The Governor's wife seems incapable of a single unselfish feeling. Vain and arrogant, she abandons her child for the sake of her own safety, then wants him back only for the wealth he can bring.

Lavrenti Vashnadze

Grusha's brother has generous instincts, but he is a cautious and conventional man, very much influenced by his wife. He is therefore glad of an opportunity to arrange for Grusha to be married and off his hands.

Simon Shashava

Grusha's devoted lover is a rather simple man who does his duty and wants out of life only a modest kind of happiness with Grusha. He is naturally distressed when it looks as though Grusha has been unfaithful to him, but he comes to her aid at the trial.

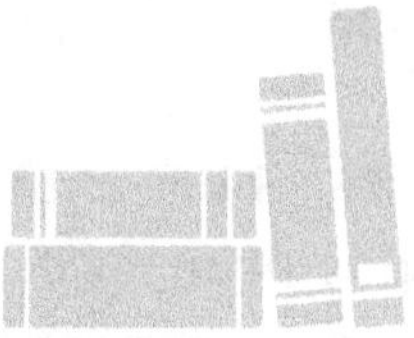

BERTOLT BRECHT

THE UNITY OF BRECHT'S WORK

Looking back over Brecht's work as a whole, we can detect in it, as in the work of any great artist, an underlying unity. This unity is not however, simple and static but complex and dynamic. It is a unity that involves both continuity and development. This may perhaps be most easily seen if we think of the relation between a few of the great characters of the later plays and their forerunners in the earlier ones. We may note, for example, that Mother Courage is a development of, and improvement upon, the character of the Widow Begbick from *A Man's A Man*. And Galileo, although a character of greater depth and complexity, is all the same a not too distant relation of Galy Gay. As for Azdak, of *The Caucasian Chalk Circle*, while retaining his own unique identity, he combines the vitality and a morality of Baal with the craftiness and adaptability of Galy Gay and Galileo.

But the pattern of unity through continuity and development is not to be found only in Brecht's characters. A similar pattern reveals itself when we examine his plays from the point of view of **theme** and technique. We find three major stages in Brecht's career. Allowing for some overlapping, the first of these covers the period from 1918 to 1929, the second covers most of the

1930s, and the third the 1940s until Brecht's move to East Berlin in 1947. From this point, Brecht shows no significant further development as a playwright but refines his work as a theoretician, especially in the *Little Organon for the Theater* (1949), and his technique as a director in his work with the Berliner Ensemble.

The first stage of Brecht's career is characterized by a philosophical nihilism reflected in technical experimentation as well as in the context of the plays. It is a though Brecht must reject simultaneously both traditional moral values and traditional aesthetic values. A nihilist vision cannot adequately be embodied in a form that was developed to articulate values Brecht cannot accept.

The first work of this period, and Brecht's first play, is *Baal* (1918), a loosely constructed play following the exploits of a central figure of immense vitality and absolute moral irresponsibility. Brecht's second play, *Drums in the Night* (1919), bears a superficial resemblance to the work of his second period, since it introduces some of the political concerns that will dominate that period. But this play is essentially antipolitical. Its hero, Andreas Kragler, rejects the revolutionary spirit he finds in postwar Berlin in favor of a life of immediate pleasures such as drink and sex.

In the Swamp (1921-24) is probably the most bitter play from this period of Brecht's career. The universe Brecht creates in *In the Swamp* is so devoid of human warmth that enmity, which at least requires some kind of contact, becomes desirable. But, in the play's despairing conclusion, even a meaningful enmity proves unattainable. In *A Man's a Man* Brecht's nihilism takes a comic turn as he recounts the transformation of Galy Gay into Jeraiah Jip. The harsh implication of this broadly funny play is that identities are easily transferable; the individual human personality is of no real value.

In *The Threepenny Opera* (1928) and *The Rise and Fall of the City of Mahagonny* (1928-29), both written in collaboration with the composer Kurt Weill, Brecht attempts to create a new musical theater to replace the traditional opera, which he described as "culinary" and regarded as dead.

By the time of Brecht's collaborations with Weill, the seeds of his second period were already being planted. He had begun to study the Socialist and Marxist theories that were to shape so much of his later thinking. Thus in *The Threepenny Opera* and *Mahagonny* Brecht attempts not only to create a new kind of musical theater but also to express a critique of bourgeois society. But the absence of a positive point of view in these works relates them to the earlier nihilistic plays and helps to explain why many audiences are entertained by the Brecht-Weill collaborations without being at all aware of their critical intentions.

After *Mahagonny* Brecht enters what we are calling his second period. Now committed to a Communist point of view, he writes works that are more relentlessly **didactic** than anything that has come before. The message of both *The Baden Cantata of Acquiescence* (1929) and *Saint Joan of the Stockyards* (1929-30) is a rejection of individual act so charity on grounds that they merely disguise the necessity of a full revolution. The point is pushed even further in *The Measures Taken* (1930). According to this play, we must be prepared to abandon not only individual acts of charity, but our very will and personality for the revolutionary cause. Ideas first presented comically in *A Man's a Man* are now presented with a new seriousness and in a new intellectual framework that makes of the denial of personality a positive good.

Throughout the 1930s Brecht, inspired by his new point of view, attempts to deal directly with the issues of his time. The attempt is only partially successful. His *Mother* (1930-32), adapted from a novel by Maxim Gorky, fails in so far as it attempts a portrayal of Russia and the Russian character. The plays that follow it are most successful when they concentrate on the particularities of character and situation; they fail when they try to grapple with larger issues.

Brecht's most aberrant play in its **theme** is *The Roundheads and the Peakheads* (1932-34), which suggests that Nazis and rich Jews are natural allies. This suggestion becomes horribly ironic in the light of the murder of six million Jews by the Nazis. *The Private Life of the Master Race* (1935-38) has some powerful moments but is naive in its approach to economic and political matters. *The Resistible Rise of Arturo Ui* (1941) is an imaginative play, but most critics find Brecht's analogy between Nazism and Chicago's gangsterism superficial. Perhaps the most successful play of this entire period is Senora Carrar's *Rifles* (1937), dealing with the Spanish Civil War. It may be significant that this play attempts less than the others to grapple with the major issues of the day, but deals persuasively with conflicts on a more personal scale.

The last important stage of Brecht's career overlaps in time with the preceding one. *Arturo Ui* (1941) belongs for its **theme** with the earlier plays, while *Mother Courage* (1938-39) and *Galileo* (first version 1937-39) are clearly of Brecht's last period. The difference is both thematic and structural. Instead of the **didactic** emphasis of the middle period, Brecht turns to a dramatic, potentially tragic, question: how can the good man survive in a cruel and hostile universe? It is the ambiguity of Brecht's answer that gives these plays their tragic dimension.

For Mother Courage, the price of endurance is constant suppression of her good instincts. Her daughter Kattrin, who acts on her good instincts, is abused, raped, and finally killed. Galileo survives to complete his scientific work only because of the cowardice that prevents him from resisting the Inquisition.

In two important plays of this period, Brecht deals with "divided" characters. In *The Good Woman of Setzuan*, Shen Te can survive only through the assistance of her imaginary cousin, Shui Ta.

In *Herr Puntila and His Man Matti* (1940), Puntila is kind and friendly when drunk, surly and selfish when sober. His goodness can reveal itself only when drink has led him to lower his guard.

Finally, in *The Caucasian Chalk Circle* (1943-45), Grusha, for all her strength, courage, and dedication, is able to survive only because of the whims of the unpredictable Azdak, and Azdak, who is frequently in danger of arrest and even of hanging, must make full use of his resources of vitality, craftiness, and adaptability.

These last plays are also distinguished from their predecessors by their abundance of unforgettably vivid characters, from Mother Courage to Adzak. But, once again, we remind ourselves that these very characters are refinements and developments of earlier Brechtian creations, and we recognize once and for all the essential unity of Brecht's work.

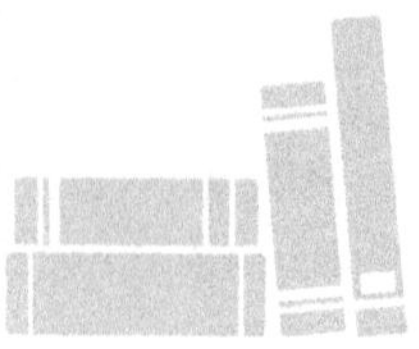

BERTOLT BRECHT

CRITICAL COMMENTARY

INTEREST IN BRECHT

Although Brecht has been dead for almost a decade, there is still relatively little significant criticism of his work in English. But the increased interest in Brecht, indicated in the United States by the recent off-Broadway productions of *The Threepenny Opera, A Man's a Man, Mother Courage*, and *Baal* and in Canada by the North American premiere of *The Rise and Fall of the City of Mahagonny* scheduled for the summer of 1965 at Stratford, Ontario, gives us reason to hope that more substantial critical study is to come.

IMPORTANT CRITICISM IN ENGLISH

Up to the present Eric Bentley has probably done more than any other single critic to arouse the interest of the English-speaking audience, especially in the United States, in the works of Brecht. In addition to the critical discussions contained in his books *The Playwright as Thinker* (1946) and *In Search of Theatre* (1953), Bentley has been involved in both amateur and professional productions of Brecht's plays. Bentley has also written introductions to a number of the plays. Valuable as it is, Bentley's criticism has its limitations. So far at least Bentley has acted as an enthusiast introducing his readers to the delights of an artist whose greatness he takes for granted.

Three important books devoted to Brecht have appeared in English. Martin Esslin's *Brecht: The Man and His Work* is an extremely valuable study, although, some may feel, more for what it says of the man than of the work. Esslin is particularly interested in the relation of Brecht's Communism to his art and in the **theme** of the conflict between reason and instinct in Brecht's work. He argues that Brecht's plays often fail to fulfill his stated intentions, but that this failure is one source of their greatness. John Willett's *The Theatre of Bertolt Brecht* treats Brecht's work from eight different aspects: subject matter, language, theatrical influences, music, theatrical practice, theory, politics, and the English aspect. Willett's approach does not permit him to enter into extended discussions of the individual plays or to offer a unified evaluation of Brecht's work as a whole.

The nearest thing to a full-length critical study, in the usual sense, that we have is Ronald Gray's *Bertolt Brecht*. Gray offers extended critical analyses and evaluations of the plays and of Brecht's theories. He argues that Brecht is at his best in five later plays: *Mother Courage, Galileo, Herr Puntila and his Man Matti, The Good Woman of Setzuan* and *The Caucasian Chalk Circle*. Gray praises Brecht for "the intensity of his probing into moral and social problems, the wisdom which shows itself in his willingness to utilize every condition and limitation of the theater in such a way as to reflect immediately on the conditions and limitations of living, the purification of his compassion from self-flattering benevolence to matter-of-fact cognizance of human needs, and the abundant vitality of many of his central characters."

Few English and American critics have risen to challenge the prevailing belief in Brecht's greatness. In his article "Of Poor Bert Brecht," however, Hubert Luethy argues that Brecht fails as a playwright and is more important for his work as a director.

OTHER CRITICISM

Much of the most important criticism of Brecht has been written in German. Ernst Schumacher's *Die dramatischen Versuche Bertolt Brechts 1918-1933* (1955) deals with Brecht's earlier plays. Schumacher places Brecht's work in the context of modern German drama and evaluates it from a Marxist point of view. Other important studies have been written by Reinhold Grimm and Walter Hinck. Some of the most important shorter essays on Brecht have been translated and included in a collection of critical essays edited by Peter Demetz.

COMMUNIST REACTIONS TO BRECHT

Schumacher's book, referred to above, is one of the few satisfactory studies of Brecht written from the Communist point of view. This may seem strange when one considers that Brecht may be the greatest Communist writer of the century, but the unorthodox nature of Brecht's plays has made them suspect in Communist countries. In fact, at the time of his death, Brecht was little known in the Soviet Union. In recent years, as part of the general thaw behind the Iron Curtain, Brecht has come to be more appreciated in the East, but some hesitancy persists. The essay by the Soviet critic I. Fradkin, available in the Demetz collection, expresses the ambivalent attitude that still seems to prevail.

SUMMARY

Interest in Brecht has never been more intense than it is now. Brecht's plays are produced in the theaters and studied in the academies. Both in the East and in the West, he is regarded as one of the most fascinating figures in the modern theater. We are perhaps still too close to him to arrive at a final evaluation of his work, but there can be no doubt that he has been a major force in the modern drama.

BERTOLT BRECHT

ESSAY QUESTIONS AND ANSWERS

THE THREEPENNY OPERA

Question: What are some of the reasons that audiences often overlook the critique of bourgeois society intended in *The Threepenny Opera?*

Answer: The first answer that comes to mind is the makeup of the theatrical audience. From the time of the first performance of *The Threepenny Opera* to the present, the theater has always depended heavily on the support of the very middle class Brecht is attacking. It is not surprising if this audience tends to be blind to its own faults and therefore to the critical implications of Brecht's work. But to some extent Brecht himself is responsible for the audience's confusion. *The Threepenny Opera* has no consistent, unifying point of view to serve as a standard of critical judgment. At times the attack seems to be directed against lack of compassion. But just as often it is suggested that life is meaningless after all; and if this is true, compassion is as meaningless as any other value. In short, Brecht's ironies in this work tend to cancel one another out. As a result, audiences find it easy to regard the play as irresponsible amusement, with little relevance to real life.

Question: What are some "alienation effects" employed in *The Threepenny Opera?*

Answer: The most striking "alienation effects" are probably found in the beggars' rehearsals of the parts they are to play, and in Peachum's demonstrations of the right way to play these parts. As we see the hideous props assembled, the gait and manner perfected, we are reminded by indirection or "alienation" of the real suffering that exists in the world. Another "alienation effect" is discovered in Peachum's complaints about the difficulties involved in arousing human pity. Peachum's cold, businesslike approach to this problem shocks us into awareness of man's true lack of compassion for his fellow man. Finally, our recognition of the similarity between the attitudes of Brecht's disreputable characters and the middle-class attitudes we have been taught to revere since childhood alienates us from the latter attitudes and forces us to examine them critically.

Question: What is the function of the music in *The Threepenny Opera?*

Answer: Brecht's attitude toward the role of music in the theater may be described as anti-Wagnerian. In his operas Richard Wagner, the nineteenth-century German composer, sought to produce a kind of hypnotic effect, overpowering the audience through music until they were unable to resist the desired emotional impact. Brecht, on the other hand, wants his audience to remain intellectually alert. His inspiration is the popular, lowbrow music of the street singer and the music hall. Within the general framework of this deliberately less than overpowering music, Brecht seeks to invite the audience's critical response by making the music comment on the action. Thus, in the "Moritat" the listing of Macheath's heinous crimes is set to a melody of dead pan monotony. The sentimental portions of the "Jealousy Duet" are set to a shallow and sugary melody that raises questions about the nature of the feelings claimed by Polly and Lucy. Instead of reinforcing and intensifying the content of the words, the music comments critically on that content.

MOTHER COURAGE

Question: How does this play illustrate Brecht's ambiguous attitude toward the traditional virtues?

Answer: It is the consistently held position of the mature Brecht that most of those human qualities we admire as virtues are signs of the imperfection of the world and would no longer be relevant in the better world of which he dreams. In this play a number of characters, including Mother Courage herself, argue that it is only in wartime that men are truly virtuous: in times of peace and prosperity they go to seed. That is, it is only because of brutality and competition among men that virtues such as courage are needed. Galileo makes a similar point in his argument with the Little Monk, and this is the meaning of Galileo's observation, "Unhappy the land that needs a hero." At the same time, Brecht must recognize that in the imperfect world in which we live, such virtues as courage and compassion, so rarely found, are to be highly valued. Thus he presents the heroic and compassionate sacrifice of Kattrin without irony.

Question: What final attitude does Brecht seem to have intended us to take toward Mother Courage?

Answer: While his comments and revisions make perfectly clear that Brecht feared audiences tended to regard Mother Courage with too much sympathy, there is no reason to conclude that he regarded all sympathy for her as misplaced. Rather, he seems to have regarded her as a complex figure demanding a complex response. Her resourcefulness and endurance, both qualities Brecht seems to value, are real, and if she is at least partly responsible for the loss of her children, her grief at their loss is certainly genuine. The complexity of Brecht's creation is perhaps most clearly illustrated by the last scene of the play. We must be moved by Mother Courage's grief, by her pathetic pretense that Kattrin may still be alive, by her lullaby. Yet even the lullaby is ambiguous, for in the sentiments expressed we see traces of Mother Courage's old selfishness. And when she hitches herself to her wagon to follow the soldiers once more she is at once pathetic in her loss, heroic in her endurance, and blind and foolish in her continued pursuit of profit from the war that has cost her so much.

GALILEO

Question: What is the relation between Galileo's virtues and his weaknesses?

Answer: Galileo's great act of weakness is, of course, his recantation, the result not of torture but merely of his being shown the instruments of torture. This is, bluntly, an act of cowardice. But it is a cowardice that grows out of Galileo's overwhelming hunger for life, a hunger that makes him peculiarly unfit to resist the threat of torture and death for the sake of an abstract principle. But it is ironic - or perhaps tragic - that it is this same hunger that drives Galileo to his scientific inquiries. In short, the same quality of his personality drives Galileo both to his cowardice and to his triumph.

Question: What moral judgments of Galileo are implied in the play?

Answer: A series of judgments of *Galileo* are offered in the play. Immediately after his recantation, Galileo is condemned by Andrea and implicity defends himself when he says, "Unhappy the land that needs a hero." But in **Scene Thirteen**, when it is known Galileo has finished Discorsi, Andrea absolves him of guilt. The ultimate value of science is contribution, and Galileo has contributed. Now Galileo condemns himself. If he had the courage to take a stand, he says, an age of reason could have been inaugurated. Obviously, conflicting moral standards are being applied, and each standard has its value. Our judgment of Galileo must recognize the complexity of his personality and his situation, but we must recognize that Brecht did not intend Galileo's adaptability to be regarded as the highest virtue.

Question: What is the relation between Galileo and Brecht?

Answer: One can never be certain about the relation between an artist and his imaginative creations, but some critics have seen in Galileo a self-portrait of his creator. They note that Brecht, too, faced his inquisitions, that of the House Un-American Activities Committee in the United States and that of the repressive East German government. In each case Brecht proved willing to make a public show of cooperation with the authorities, where others might have felt an unequivocal moral stand was called for. Brecht may have felt that, for him as for Galileo, an attitude of adaptability was required if he was to be allowed to continue with his work. At the same time, Brecht, who was capable of imagining a Joan Dark, a Kattrin, a Grusha, may have been aware of the unheroic side of his own behavior. The creation of *Galileo* may then have been an attempt by Brecht to externalize his own moral conflicts.

THE GOOD WOMAN OF SETZUAN

Question: Is it proper to regard Shen Te as the embodiment of a moral ideal?

Answer: In evaluating the moral significance of any character from Brecht's later plays, one must keep in mind Brecht's constant employment of a double vision in these works. That is, the characters must be seen in the light of the imperfect world that does exist and of the better world that Brecht hopes will come to exist. In the real and imperfect world Shen Te's passive goodness provides an inadequate model, as her dependence on Shui Ta implies. In this world, the more tolerant and realistic code proposed by Wong the Water Seller is probably preferable. But Brecht's dream is of a world in which Shen Te could survive happily without the assistance of Shui Ta. In that sense, she suggests Brecht's moral ideal, but it is an ideal by which society, rather than the individual, is to be judged.

Question: What is the relation between this play and Brecht's theory of alienation?

Answer: The purpose of the alienation effect is to force us to see things in a new light, thereby encouraging us to examine them critically and ask if they must be as they are. It may be said that alienation, in this sense, is the basic strategy of this entire play. The division of the **protagonist** into Shen Te and Shui Ta makes us see in a new light the often contradictory relation between moral professions and practical behavior. The presence of the gods, mouthing moralistic slogans, makes us question the value of the very principles these absurd figures find is so easy to express. We are, in short, alienated from our conventional moral assumptions and made to subject them to critical re-examination.

THE CAUCASIAN CHALK CIRCLE

Question: In what sense are the judgments of Azdak consistent with Brecht's moral concerns?

Answer: Like Brecht, Azdak finds little meaning in conventional notions of guilt and innocence. These are too narrowly limited to judgments of the individual, when it is society that needs to be judged. Therefore, Azdak can proceed freely, with no apparent concern for the application of rational standards of judgment. Yet one notes that he always decides in favor of the victim of society, for example the old woman who has received meat from a bandit and, of course, Grusha herself. This is why the period of his judging is finally considered an age almost of justice.

Question: What structural problems does the play present?

Answer: The play attempts to deal with three different stories: the framework story, the story of Grusha, and the story of Azdak. The question is whether Brecht succeeds in making a unified play out of these materials. Few critics would defend the Prologue, either in itself or in its relation to the play as a whole. Yet it does introduce the Story Teller, who acts as a chorus and, by his comments, serves to alienate the action. To devote an entire act to the story of Azdak just as the story of Grusha is reaching its height is, to put it mildly, unconventional dramatic technique. But we must see this deviation from the norm in the light of Brecht's purpose. It is not enough for him that we become emotionally involved in Grusha's story, as we are at the end of **Act Three**. And this involvement would certainly deepen, possibly at the expense of intellectual awareness, if we went from the capture of the child to the trial itself. **Act Four**, besides introducing us to one of the most memorable of Brecht's characters, creates a diversion from this deepening emotional involvement and permits the reawakening of the intellectual faculties. It also extends the meaning of the trial itself, and therefore of Grusha's story as a whole, by showing us the disordering of circumstances that is necessary if a good poor woman like Grusha is to win out over her evil rich enemies.

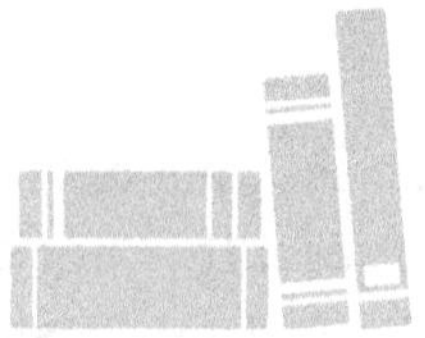

BIBLIOGRAPHY

This bibliography attempts to list only the most important items readily available in English to the American student.

Abel, Lionel. *Metatheatre: A New View of Dramatic Form*. New York, 1963. Two chapters on Brecht in a work that attempts to define significant trends in the modern theater.

Adler, Henry. "Bert Brecht's Theatre," *The Twentieth Century* 160 (1956), 114-123.

Bentley, Eric. *In Search of Theatre*. New York, 1953. An important chapter on Brecht's stagecraft.

_____. "Introduction," *Seven Plays by Bertolt Brecht*. Stimulating discussions of seven of the plays analyzed in this study guide.

_____. *The Playwright as Thinker*. New York, 1946. One of the important critical studies of the modern drama; last chapter deals with Brecht.

Brecht on Theatre, trans. John Willett. New York, 1964. A selection of Brecht's theoretical writings.

Brustein, Robert. *The Theatre of Revolt: An Approach to the Modern Drama*. New York, 1964. One chapter on Brecht, emphasizing the element of "revolt" in his work. The book as a whole is invaluable to the student of modern drama.

Demetz, Peter, ed. *Brecht: A Collection of Critical Essays*. New York, 1962. Includes a number of essays newly translated into English.

Esslin, Martin. *Brecht: The Man and His Work*. New York, 1960. A critical biography.

Fergusson, Francis. *The Human Image in Dramatic Literature*. New York, 1957. One chapter on Brecht, Wilder, and Eliot as modern allegorists.

Garten, H. F. *Modern German Drama*. New York, 1962. A historical survey, with one chapter on Brecht.

Gorelik, Mordecai. *New Theatres for Old*. New York, 1962. A study of theatre by a friend and colleague of Brecht; contains many references to Brecht's theory and practice.

Gray, Ronald. *Bertolt Brecht*. New York, 1961. A concise and useful general introduction.

Luethy, Herbert. "Of Poor Bert Brecht," *Encounter* 34 (July, 1956), 33-53. Unsympathetic to some elements of Brecht's work and character.

Willett, John. *The Theatre of Bertolt Brecht: A Study from Eight Aspects*. New York, 1954. A valuable, informative handbook.

www.ingramcontent.com/pod-product-compliance
Lightning Source LLC
Chambersburg PA
CBHW061504050726
47593CB00002B/444

* 9 7 8 1 6 4 5 4 2 4 2 4 6 *